WHAT I HATE ABOUT FOOTBALL

About the Author

Richard Foster is formerly of the Financial Times and has written for The Football League as well as a variety of football websites. He also writes on football and other aspects of life for Sabotagetimes.com. He can be found online at www.azfootballhates.co.uk.

WHAT I HATE ABOUT FOOTBALL

Richard Foster

AMBERLEY

Images 1–3 and 5–7 courtesy of the Press Association. Image 4 courtesy of Historical Football Kits.

First published 2014
This edition published 2016

Amberley Publishing
The Hill, Stroud
Gloucestershire, GL5 4EP

www.amberley-books.com

British Library Cataloguing in Publication Data.
A catalogue record for this book is available from the British Library.

ISBN 978 1 4456 5537 6 (paperback)
ISBN 978 1 4556 3993 2 (ebook)

Typeset in 11pt on 12pt Sabon.
Typesetting and Origination by Amberley Publishing.
Printed in the UK.

Contents

Foreword

Hatred is an emotive and challenging subject. The strongest, deepest hate is usually inspired by love, and so it is with this book, *What I Hate about Football.* My passion for football is almost limitless; just ask my wife. I have been to well over 500 games, have spent thousands of hours watching televised matches and like nothing more than nattering on about football. In addition to this, I have played football for almost fifty years and am still playing every week without fail. I cannot get enough of it.

However, out of this unwavering attachment to the sport over five decades I have developed a series of gripes and grumbles, and these are what have inspired the idea of assembling this collection of hates. Indeed, when I first alighted on the concept, I scribbled down eighty-seven specific hates about the game I love so much. These hates do not in any way diminish my love of the game; they colour and characterise it. This is also not an attempt to scoff at the modern game, as that has been done very successfully before. Many of the dislikes featured here have their roots further back, in the colourful 1960s, the dour 1970s or the blighted 1980s.

There is no simple dichotomy between the good old times and the rotten contemporary ones. Some would have you believe that there is a mystical line drawn around 1969 that divides the history of English football; the days where behatted crowds waved rattles furiously, revelling in Stanley Matthews' deft skills as he danced down the wing were replaced seemingly overnight by those times when the terracing was awash with rampaging hooligans watching overpaid, pampered prima donnas indulging in monotonous hoofball. But, in reality, there were some major imperfections in those heady days and while there is much to admonish today, there is also plenty to admire. This is, therefore, a look at both the inglorious past and the ignoble present, as well as a disconcerting peek into the nightmarish future.

Today, we have to endure the trend of players openly and unashamedly taking 'selfie' photographs. This is not only an exercise in vanity but also a prime illustration of how technology can make things much worse. Twitter has given us access to far too much information, and the series of faux pas, badly judged comments and general drivel spilling out courtesy of social media is part of the communication overload that has affected all our lives, and not just the world of football. But I am sure that if George Best or Jimmy Greaves had had such access we would have been treated to some pretty tawdry nonsense.

So the original eighty-seven hates were liberally scattered across the decades, but they were entirely subjective and highly personal choices. In order to make something that would be more attractive to the wider public, I set out to gather others' views and opinions. I was delighted to find that nearly everyone I spoke to, from all walks of life, immediately understood the concept behind the book and were more than willing to share their own bugbears. There is a pervading sense of catharsis in the process of sharing hates and releasing our demons.

One of the more idiosyncratic selections – and, as a result of its quirkiness, one of my favourites – was the choice of Steve, a long-suffering Chester fan. Steve has witnessed his club's decline over the last ten years or so, as they fell from being a stable Football League club into a basket case, losing their sixty-nine-year-old grip on League status in 2000. Despite coming back up four years later, the writing was on the wall; massive financial difficulties and a rapid turnover of managers finally led to the winding-up of Chester City in 2010 as they were expelled from the Conference Premier. Their reinvention as plain old Chester FC within a few months of their demise saw Chester climbing back up the league pyramid, having secured three successive promotions. Alas, this season Chester slipped out of the Conference Premier in the last five minutes of the last league match on goal difference (they subsequently won a reprieve from relegation in the close season when Hereford United were expelled from the League).

Steve and fellow Chester fans have certainly been through the mill, and have been scarred by the whole topsy-turvy experience, as was reflected in his rather off-the-wall hatred, namely that of home matches. For the majority of supporters, when clubs play at home, it is an advantage to be enjoyed – but not for Steve. He cannot stand the expectation of winning, which is naturally bestowed on the team playing on its own ground. As Chester have repeatedly let him down so badly in the past, hope has been replaced by a grim fatalism that something will go wrong, and invariably it does.

Understanding Steve's fear and apprehension reveals much of the psyche of the football fan, and is a wonderful insight into the world of football and its rich mixture of hates, particularly from someone who has been shuffled around at the bottom of the pile for a while. This is not the whingeing of a fan whose team has failed to qualify for the Champions League or has not won a trophy for a few years, but the real concern of someone who has watched his club disappear and then return in another guise. This type of situation is where loyalty shows its colours, and hates are chosen with a perspective that is born out of survival, not just glory hunting. His pain is tangible and his hate is heartfelt. His first match was Chester 2 Darlington 1, Third Division, 17 March 1984, attendance 981. Little did he know what the future might hold.

You're supposed to be at home – Steve Hill

As a cash-strapped youth living within walking distance of the old ground, home games were the bread and butter of the season. Rarely missed, it wasn't unusual to get in for 2 p.m., flick through the programme, watch the players warm up, and simply soak up the atmosphere. Win, lose or draw, you'd be home in time for the *Brookside* omnibus, or even sooner with a pack of feral away fans at your heel.

Some decades later, decamped 200 miles away from a modern sterile stadium, home fixtures are a far more onerous business. A Groundhog Day of M6 road works, a snatched pint, and a speck stood amid the same old serial moaners, it feels like a chore as opposed to the gleeful jaunt of a decent away day.

It wouldn't be so bad if there were ever anything like a good atmosphere. It's a strange truism that 10 to 20 per cent of the home crowd travel away, yet manage to make considerably more noise. Home games are too often a stifled affair, with the weight of expectation transferring to the team, resulting in nervy, halting performances.

As Morrissey once pointed out, when you lose in front of your home crowd, you wish the ground would open up and take you down. A bit strong, perhaps, but there are few worse feelings than the trudge to the car following a home defeat. It's not unheard of for nobody to speak until at least Birmingham, at which point somebody will emit a heartfelt 'fuck's sake!' and start flicking through the programme to find the next away game.

Steve's torment encapsulates the very essence of individual agony that is at the heart of being a fan; it is deeply personal and painful, but cannot be resisted. There is no antidote, just more pain heaped on top of existing pain. Like Steve's, many of the featured hates are highly personal, touching a raw nerve and one that true football fans can immediately recognise. There are other hates, which are less individual; these are more generic but equally impassioned.

Take the mid-winter break as a prime example. It comes up as a topic of discussion every year and then gets buried away as quickly as it has gained prominence. For one week it is top of the agenda, and there is little else that is talked about. The ritual begins when a couple of Conference matches are postponed, then switches to full-on crisis mode as a League Two match falls foul of the weather. Cue mass hysteria, and the first calls for a mid-winter break begin to be heard above the screams of impending disaster. It represents the perfect storm for a media frenzy, combining as it does our two national obsessions of weather and football.

The next stage in the national crisis is triggered when the mysterious Pools Panel is asked to move in. Once the country is put on red alert and the rising clamour for a mid-winter break is in full flow, the evidence is waved in front of our faces: Germany. The sole reason its national team has held the whip hand over England over the last forty-eight years is because they allow their players a couple of weeks off during the height of winter. Bayern Munich and Borussia Dortmund are at the apex of European club football because their players are as fresh as daisies between January and May. The FA is implored to follow the German example, with the promise that all this country's football ills will be swept away once fixtures are scheduled to include a winter break.

To stumble across the panacea is hailed as a godsend – other countries such as Italy, Spain and France have adopted the idea, and *they* have done pretty well out of it, so it is surely full steam ahead. That is, until somebody points to a notable exception, which takes the wind out of everyone's sails. One country did introduce a mid-winter break, but has not made such an impact on the world stage in recent years. In fact, it has not even reached a major tournament since 1998. With eight successive qualifying failures behind them, the Scots have well and truly blown the idea that a break will be of benefit to the nation's football.

Watching the odd minute of Scottish league action does not instil too much confidence in the system per se, unless the struggles of plucky Kilmarnock and St Johnstone keeping up with all-conquering Celtic are anything to go by. So it is back to the drawing board, and a few more sessions of head scratching, some blue-sky thinking and a cold dose of reality – by which time the thaw has kicked in and all is forgotten for another year.

Some hates are not seasonal but they are with us all year round. Former cricketer Simon Hughes, aka The Analyst, makes the case against football in general. Having discovered that football has morphed into something else, Hughes does not hold back in his invective, and he has shunned the game ever since.

Simon Hughes, broadcaster and author, on how football turned him off

I hate people asking me what team I support. I hate it even more when I answer 'no one', and they look at me in amazement as if it is compulsory to support a football team if you are a bloke. Well, I don't support anyone, okay? And I have no desire to, either, since Premiership footballers are overpaid and underwhelming. I can't bear all their posturing and abuse, particularly of referees. Their behaviour is appalling, totally arrogant and disrespectful. It's not how sport should be.

I did support a team once. I was a passionate follower of Spurs in the 1970s in the days of Pat Jennings, Martin Chivers, Mike England and Cyril Knowles – White Hart Lane was where the phrase 'nice one Cyril!' was coined. Most of the lads who played pro football then seemed quite decent (as opposed to the fans), and I went to most home matches for about five years.

But as soon as I started going abroad to play cricket in the winter, I lost touch with Spurs and professional football. When I was back one winter in the late 1980s, footballers had changed into these angry, arrogant, overpaid exhibitionists. They had lost touch with sport and the real world. They lived this rarefied life surrounded by agents and entourages and sycophants. I wasn't interested in their world any more, and have never regained any affection for it.

Perhaps what I hate most of all is the blind loyalty shown by otherwise quite intelligent people to their football club, in spite of a) the lack of skill and success

> of their team, b) the greedy attitudes of the clubs towards the fans and c) the disgusting behaviour of some of the players. Football seems to breed a kind of indoctrination of normal, decent people, who turn into foul-mouthed apologists for players with very little ability and even less integrity, and I am glad it never captured me.

Simon was taken to his first match, Chelsea *v.* Leeds at Stamford Bridge, by the local vicar with his sons in around 1969. From a quasi-religious baptism, Hughes eventually turned his back on football and has never returned. He is one of the few contributors who have done so, with the vast majority still enamoured by the game but irritated by its many foibles and faults.

The actor Christopher Eccleston went to his first match a few years after Hughes, on 11 October 1973, to see Manchester United lose 2-1 at home to Bristol Rovers in a League Cup tie. Like Hughes, Eccleston questions the players' motivation and their disregard for the fans. Worryingly, he suggests that this might prevent future generations from going to matches.

> **The players aren't playing for the manager – Christopher Eccleston**
>
> How about the players play for their wages? For personal pride? For the shirt that they so often kiss? For the memory of the players who, on a minimum wage, created the foundations of the club that now employs them? For the man or woman who has supported the club with his

time and money for fifty years or more? For the eight-year-old whose first ever football match it is? For the man or woman who forked out seventy quid for a ticket and a hundred quid for rail fare or petrol?

And if they could manage to not dive, simulate or cheat while they do it, I might actually want to take my son to a game.

Having been overwhelmed by suggestions from those I approached, the only complication was how to whittle the vast range down to a single hate from each contributor, as the majority were spoilt for choice. Many of the choices resonated with my own, which was reassuring, but the beauty was that there were a fair few that surprised and delighted me. I have thoroughly enjoyed the whole process of assembling these for the purposes of the book. It proved to be a labour of love as well as of hate.

The hates range from the mildly irritating, through the bloody annoying and all the way to the utterly obnoxious and outrageous, but nearly all of them are born out of love. So whether they are the sort of thing that raises a smile of acknowledgement, or are aspects of the game that have you waking up in the middle of the night screaming, they all belong here. The whole gamut is included, from conniving ball boys to supposedly mature, sane adults dressed as six-foot farmyard animals, from the disturbing machinations of FIFA to the mourning of the loss of the genuine drop-ball. This is one part celebration to nine parts lament.

As Chrissie Hynde pointed out in the mid-1980s,

there certainly is a thin line between love and hate, and this book treads it very carefully. It has been a delicate balancing act, which may at times topple over into one camp but soon hops back into the other. The primary aim is to amuse and entertain, rather than to antagonise and annoy. So hopefully nobody will take offence and accept it in good heart, as it was intended.

Welcome to *What I Hate about Football*, and I hope you love reading it as much as I did writing it.

A is for Agents

Come, seeling night,
Scarf up the tender eye of pitiful day;
And with thy bloody and invisible hand
Cancel and tear to pieces that great bond
Which keeps me pale! Light thickens, and the crow
Makes wing to the rooky wood:
Good things of day begin to droop and drowse;
While night's black agents to their preys do rouse.
From *Macbeth* by William Shakespeare

Nobody is quite sure when agents first appeared on the football scene, but they are about as welcome a guest as Banquo's ghost was to Macbeth. It is difficult to imagine quite how unpopular agents are with the vast majority of the football fraternity. Having been described as leeches, parasites and bloodsuckers by all and sundry, there is little room for much doubt. They are the pantomime villains of the football industry; as soon as they appear, there are boos and howls of derision, which only die down once they disappear out of view, returning to the underworld where they belong. Football is generally a divisive landscape in which opinions vary enormously, but if there is one thing that unites everybody, it is a hatred of agents.

Simon Jordan was particularly virulent about them and their pernicious influence over the game in his autobiography *Be Careful What You Wish For*, when he did not hold back in his condemnation of that loathsome breed. He described one as looking like a cross 'between Ming the Merciless and Dick Dastardly', and he sums up what he sees as a one-way street. 'It still bemuses me,' Jordan writes, 'why the only people in football who pay nothing yet earn out of it are agents.' His damning conclusion takes no prisoners. 'To my mind, on the whole agents were little better than skin traders and it was incumbent on the football authorities to control this unnecessary evil that, in my view, served no greater good.'

Indeed, Jordan refused to sanction the transfer of Tim Cahill, who could have made the difference to Crystal Palace's survival chances in 2004/05, because the agent was demanding too high a fee, reputedly in the region of £150,000. So Cahill went to Everton, where he became a prolific scorer, while Palace were relegated by one point on the last day of the season. I and many Palace fans were therefore in agreement with Jordan, maybe for the first and only time, in being dead against agents and their wicked ways, although we would not go as far as Jordan's recommendation via his *Observer* column that 'all agents should be neutered'.

Who will stand up for these poor souls? Well, it took a while to find anyone willing to defend them; even one agent, who wished to remain nameless for obvious reasons, agreed that they were a despicable bunch. Untrustworthy and universally abhorred, they do not have many standing up in their defence. We may not agree on very much, but those agents are truly the lowest of the low. There is a fundamental mistrust of middlemen who cream off money from transfers and seem hell-bent on agitating moves for their clients so that they can generate more income for themselves. It is in the agent's interest to engineer as many moves as possible. Loyalty (see 'L is for Loyalty') is not rewarded; in fact, it is actively discouraged, as that would not be good for business. Jumping from club to club is much better, and there are plenty of players who have become serial transfer fodder, mainly through the exhortations of you-know-who.

Typical of the brinksmanship that gives them such a bad name were the machinations of Nicolas Anelka's agent, Claude, who also happened to be his brother. Claude was instrumental in Anelka's acrimonious departure from Arsenal in 1999. Having stated publicly that Anelka would be staying at Arsenal, within a few months his tune had changed considerably, as a variety of clubs, including Lazio and Real Madrid, started to court the French striker's signature. 'Arsenal must hurry if they want to conclude a deal,' Claude said. 'If not, Nicolas will stay a year without playing. That's no problem.' This was standard behaviour, and eventually Anelka secured his move to Real Madrid and Claude was no doubt busy counting his share of £23.5 million deal. No problem, Claude.

The history of agents dates back to the early days of professional football when they were used to help build teams such as Middlesbrough Ironopolis from scratch, and jolly useful they were too. After the introduction of the maximum wage in 1900 their use diminished almost overnight and they disappeared from the domestic scene for a while, only occasionally popping up to facilitate British players moving abroad.

Breaking the mould was Bagnal Harvey, who was introduced to the very first poster boy of English football, Denis Compton. Harvey proceeded to secure various lucrative ancillary deals for Compton, such as one of the very first product endorsements with Brylcreem. Compton was a rarity, as his fame was enhanced by both his doubling up as a cricket international and his being one of a new breed of playboys in the post-war period.

But, just as players gradually regained some control of their own destiny, back came the agents. They were led by the irrepressible Eric Hall, who left a stench of cigar smoke and his particular brand of chutzpah. His catchphrase of 'monster, monster' summed up the brazen attitude that so often alienated agents from everyone else. Wherever agents roamed, there was a lingering sense of something amiss not being too far behind them. Even some of their own have admitted that the murky world of bungs and brown envelopes is still very much alive and kicking, despite sporadic investigations into these shady goings-on.

No less a figure than the former Metropolitan Police Commissioner Lord Stevens conducted an inquiry in 2007, which had been prompted by allegations from managers Mike Newell and Ian Holloway, who claimed that illegal payments to agents were rife throughout the game. The Stevens inquiry unearthed seventeen transfers involving fifteen agents that caused concern. Clubs such as Chelsea, Newcastle, Bolton, Portsmouth and Middlesbrough were implicated, but not accused of any wrongdoing. The response of some of the agents named was suitably strong and uncompromising, such as Barry Silkman, who, with typical agent bravado, did not hold back.

> 'It's an absolute, total lie,' he thundered. 'A complete lie. Whoever he is, Lord Stevens, he is a liar. The people who have done this are liars. I challenge them now to take me to court and let them say that I've done something wrong in the Fabio Rochemback deal. I promise if they do, I will begin litigation and do everything in my power not just to close them down, but I will discredit them like you cannot believe. They will rue the day they were ever born. They are total liars.' He reiterated his threat to sue, adding: 'Every bit of money I win will go to the NSPCC.'
>
> *The Guardian*, 15 June 2007

This was a turn-up for the books; here was proof that agents had a conscience, and even evidence that some had a heart.

None of the agents involved, including Silkman, ever faced charges, and the storm created seemed to have passed by. A series of arrests followed the initial investigations, and high-profile individuals such as Harry Redknapp and Karren Brady were questioned, but nothing was proven, so football returned to its norm of rumour, insinuation and supposition.

More recently we have had 'Cakegate', when Yaya Toure's agent, Dmitri Seluk, exhibited one of the most brazen examples of chicanery. Seluk expressed his client's dismay that he only received a cake, and very little respect, from Manchester City on his thirty-first birthday. When it was suggested that this standoff might have been a negotiating ruse to squeeze out a little more from his existing contract, Seluk was defiant. 'No. Money is not important,' Seluk said. 'He has enough money. The most important thing is a human relationship, and maybe this is an opportunity for Yaya to find that. If City don't respect him then, easy, Yaya will leave. No problem. It is more important he plays for a club that respects him more than having a few thousand pounds added to his salary. I have spoken to him about leaving and we will see what happens, but, at the moment, Yaya is really upset.'

Seluk is right, of course. What is a few thousand pounds on a salary reported to be in excess of £14 million a year? Irrelevant. Playing the respect card is one of those classic tactics that suggests that moral superiority is far more important than material wealth. However, Seluk could not resist pointing out that Brazilian Roberto Carlos had once been given a Bugatti car worth £800,000 for his birthday by Russian club Anzhi. Now that is a mark of true respect.

By sowing the seeds of doubt, Seluk created that chink of uncertainty that can be exploited. He also raised the emotional stakes by letting us know that Toure was 'really upset', not that the player himself would say that, as he pointed out in a tweet. 'Everything Dmitri said is true. He speaks for me. I will explain after the World Cup.' The timing of the indignant outburst is also worth noting, just after City had won the Premier League and just weeks before the World Cup started. In some quarters, that is known as the window of opportunity – the perfect time to start upping your client's profile and attracting some suitors who value human relationships above all else and, coincidentally, can chuck in the odd birthday gift to underline the depth of their feelings and their pockets.

B is for Babies

> I am assured by a very knowing American of my acquaintance in London; that a young healthy child, well nursed, is, at a year old, a most delicious, nourishing, and wholesome food; whether stewed, roasted, baked or boiled, and I make no doubt, that it will equally serve in a fricassee, or ragout.
>
> From *A Modest Proposal* by Jonathan Swift

Whoever first dreamt up the idea of taking young children to accompany the players while they pick up their medals and lift the cup should be extradited to a very desolate and bleak island, from which there should be no return. The overt sentimentality of carrying babes in arms up the Wembley steps has now become so well entrenched that it has become part and parcel of the rigmarole surrounding the trophy ceremony.

Dennis Wise is often cited as the pioneer of the parading of offspring. It was May 2000, Chelsea had won the FA Cup with ease, and maybe Wise decided it was time to break away from the shackles of his image as a (small)

1. Dennis Wise clutches his son Henry close to him to celebrate Chelsea's 2000 FA Cup final win; thus began the tradition of parading offspring while collecting trophies.

hardman. Or maybe this was Wise wising up to the idea of a modern man, one who is comfortable with his paternal duties and shares the responsibility of being a parent, in what was the start of the twenty-first century. If that was the motivation, then fair play to Dennis, although one can only shudder at the thought of him trying to do the same in 1988 with his Wimbledon teammates, the 'Crazy Gang'. Bathwater, baby – but not necessarily in that order – would be among the milder suggestions.

Irrespective of his inspiration, Wise grabbed five-month-old Henry and tucked him under his arm as if collecting the groceries. In fact, Wise was following the schmaltzy precedent set by Scholes, Beckham and even the uncompromising Keane, all of whom had dragged their small children on to the pitch while celebrating another League title a few weeks beforehand. And thus the infant-carrying tradition was established, and its grip on the country's footballers has never been relinquished.

In fact, some miscreant footballers now see the parading of their little ones as an essential step on the path to redemption. Luis Suárez was inseparable from his baby daughter, Delfina, after he returned from his original 'Bite Ban'. She escorted him on to the pitch at several games, and it would have been no surprise if Delfina had popped up on the left side of midfield to feed her father's insatiable thirst for goals. To be even-handed, Suárez did wear an undershirt celebrating his son Benjamin's birth when he scored a couple of goals against Sunderland on his first League match back in September 2013. The Uruguayan may have more than his fair share of bad days but, underneath it all, he is a dad.

In light of Suárez's latest misdemeanours at the World Cup in Brazil, when he just could not resist a crafty nibble on Chiellini's shoulder, there is speculation about an imminent move to Barcelona from Liverpool. There will also be intense scrutiny over how he might mark his re-emergence from the four-month ban imposed by FIFA, but rest assured; the next phase of his charm offensive will feature Luis' children in and around Camp Nou as their father waits in the wings. It was significant that the most used picture of the Uruguayan after the Chiellini incident was of him holding his child while on a balcony, not unlike the famous Michael Jackson shot outside a Berlin hotel – but, crucially, Suárez was not dangling his child precariously over the edge, being a caring sort of parent.

In his belated admission of guilt, which was released via his Twitter page, there was little doubt that Suárez was yet again playing his dad card to the full. 'After several days being home with my family, I have had the opportunity to regain my calm and reflect on the reality of what occurred during the Italy–Uruguay match.' He then proceeded to apologise to 'Chiellini and the entire football family', and let's face it, who doesn't have the odd spat with a member of their family every now and again? Perhaps a display of his kids' cherubic faces on the seats alongside the Catalan side's 'Mes Que un Club' motto would be an appropriate way of welcoming the wayward striker to his new surroundings and assuring the waiting world that he is just a family man.

Tracing the history of children being involved in celebrations takes us all the way back to the 1994 World Cup in the USA, when Brazilian striker Bebeto launched the 'cradle-rocking' gesture, along with teammates Romario and Mazinho, after his goal against Netherlands in the quarter-final. The swinging-arm *bebé* routine, accompanied by inane grinning/gurning, became de rigueur for a year or two in the aftermath of *los trios amigos*' Dallas display. The rationale for this extravagant paternal show was the birth of Bebeto's son, Mattheus, just two days before the match.

The child was named after German star Lothar Matthäus and, with a custom-made on-field celebration to boot, he had much to live up to. But, to give him his due, he has since gone on to play for Flamengo and the Brazilian Under-21 side, and is no doubt brushing up on his own celebratory technique for any of his own progeny. Like father, like son. For a few years afterwards this celebration was all the rage, aped and imitated by a broad range of footballers, although it appeared a little incongruous when unveiled on a wet, windy night in Rochdale.

So, thanks to Bebeto and chums, for any lap of honour or post-season team celebration the players can hardly move for the mass of small children cavorting across the grass, as if this were some massive nursery picnic. It is as if they have to show us that they are just like us, underneath it all. Some may call this a heart-warming revelation that footballers are family men and not just money-grabbing mercenaries. But for others of a more cynical bent, it reeks of mawkish claptrap.

The presence of children on the pitch is not a recent development. The rare honour of being the club's matchday mascot is a tradition that predates the Premier League, but the experience has changed, and not necessarily for the better. What used to happen was that a single child was chosen to lead the teams out, maybe even taking part in the pre-match kick-about, and then joining the captains and referee in the centre circle for a photo opportunity. It was exclusive and it was fun. Now we are in the realms of multiple mascots, so for Premier

League matches there are mascots for every home player, and a gaggle of youngsters accompanies even the away team nowadays. The pitch resembles a wet weekend in a Wacky Warehouse, with nippers aplenty.

This may seem to be a more inclusive way of going about things, but, at the root of this, there is the issue of money. The myriad of various mascot packages available from every club across the country has reached extraordinary proportions. The general rule of thumb is that you will get fleeced for the privilege and joys of your child being one of the massed ranks of little ones paraded on the hallowed turf. Do not be fooled into thinking that this is the club showing off its family credentials; it is merely yet another way of coaxing some more money out of you.

If the sight of small children cavorting around the pitch is not enough, then there is the presence of youngsters in the stands, which can also be a major impediment to enjoyment of a game. While I understand the urge to bring your son or daughter to football as early as possible, the consequences should be heeded. There is nothing worse than being next to a child who is a) too young to understand what is going on, and b) in need of constant distraction. This usually starts after four minutes with persistent kicking of the seat in front, and when that has reached a level that can no longer be tolerated there is the pressing need to go to the loo. This brief respite is broken on their return, when the child demands sweets, drinks and general goodies as soon as they have retaken their seat.

And on it goes, until the desperate plea to be taken home, even though the second half is barely five minutes old, begins in earnest. The battle to keep the child in the ground is now well and truly joined, and takes up the next twenty-five minutes until finally the parent concedes. To mass relief from all in the vicinity, they get ready to leave, which involves a series of checks and double checks on coats and general possessions. The most chilling part of the whole affair is hearing the kid declare, 'That was fun – when's the next game?'

And then we have the thorny subject of ballboys, which has become one of those issues that has rattled quite a few cages. Although these may appear at first to be innocent bystanders, to some they are calculating demons with machinations way beyond their tender years. In the past, I have been riled by their inability to perform the simple task of returning the ball to the players. But I soon realised that this is all part of a Machiavellian plot to either slow down the game, wasting inordinate amounts of time, or to accelerate the return of the ball to such a degree that the ballboys are nearly all encroaching on the pitch in their desperation to get the ball back into play.

Just ask Eden Hazard about Swansea's Charlie Morgan, the seventeen-year-old who smothered the ball in his attempt to slow play down during a League Cup semi-final in 2013 and got a kick in the ribs for his trouble. Morgan may have been betraying his Celtic fondness for rugby, but there is no hiding the fact that Hazard overreacted and deserved his red card. However, to portray Morgan as an innocent victim is to overlook the complicity in time-wasting that night at the Liberty Stadium from the self-acclaimed king of the ballboys. This confirmed the view that ballboys have become integral instruments of team strategy rather than neutral helpers, as illustrated by the selective use of towels at Stoke, which were readily available to Rory Delap but conspicuous by their absence when the opposition were preparing to hurl projectiles into the Stoke penalty area. We cannot be too far away from the time when we see the ballboys gather in a pre-match huddle, attracting marks out of ten for their performances and being considered in the man of the match awards.

B is for Bell

> And therefore never send to know for whom the bell tolls; it tolls for thee.
>
> From 'Devotions upon Emergent Occasions'
> by John Donne

The roar of an impassioned crowd is one of the most attractive, intoxicating elements of the game, and the atmosphere at matches is one of the few things where the English can rightly claim to be towards the upper echelons of world football. Although there has been a distillation of fans' fervour (see 'C is for Corporate Hospitality') in recent times, English fans are still noisy and very much in your face. But there is one area of supporting your team to the hilt that has gone too far, and that is the flagrant use of bells by certain individuals who will now be named and shamed.

The first occasion in which I became aware of this was when travelling to Fratton Park, which is a tight, intimidating place to go at the best of times. There were Pompey fans generating an unusual noise within the overall clamour, and it sounded initially like a serious case of tinnitus but turned out to be someone ringing a bell. Of course, Pompey have had their problems in the last five years as they have scuttled down the leagues, bouncing from one shady, tight owner (see 'O is for Owners') to the next in a desperate plunge to the basement. Despite all their trials and tribulations, the supporters, who have now thankfully wrested control of the club into their own hands, have been magnificent. Unwavering loyalty in the face of such adversity is commendable. But this does not excuse the use of the bell. John 'Portsmouth Football Club' Westwood is primarily to blame as the chief bell-ringer. While we can appreciate that there is some resonance with the club anthem, 'Pompey Chimes', there is really no rhyme or reason for such flagrant use of a bell at football matches.

The much-tattooed Westwood is immediately recognisable and he clearly has Pompey running through his veins as well as all over his skin, but he does seem to have misplaced the odd screw. What possessed him to take a bell into the ground in the first place is beyond most people's comprehension, but that is indeed what he did. Not that Westwood is alone in his inappropriate campanology. Manchester City fans will remember with affection Helen 'The Bell' Turner, who rang her bell with defiant loyalty for over thirty years, but surely there are better ways of showing support for your club and not annoying the majority of right-thinking people. For many people football is a religion, but this is one step too far. Bells belong in church towers and cathedrals, not in football grounds.

C is for Corporate Hospitality

> We're 1-0 up, then there are one or two stray passes and they're getting on players' backs. It's just not on. At the end of the day, they need to get behind the team. Away from home, our fans are fantastic, I'd call them the hardcore fans. But at home, they have a few drinks and probably the prawn sandwiches, and they don't realise what's going on out on the pitch. I don't think some of the people who come to Old Trafford can spell 'football', never mind understand it.
>
> Roy Keane after Manchester United's Champions League game against Dynamo Kiev in 2000

Keane's derogatory comments about the lack of atmosphere at Old Trafford brought him further notoriety, alongside some of his more inflammatory actions and words. But there is no denying that the pugilistic, belligerent Roy was pretty much on the money with this particular verbal assault. There has been a massive shift in the matchday experience over the last few decades, and corporate hospitality sits inertly at the core of this worrying transformation.

From being essentially a working-class sport for the first hundred years of the League, football at the very top of the pyramid has become an opportunity to flex a company's global branding muscles; clubs are seen more as conduits for marketing messages rather than the heart of the local community. Sponsors circle around the clubs with the ravenous hunger of vultures, waiting to pick off the latest tasty morsel to spill out of the corporate treasure chest.

Considering that sponsorship only made a visible mark on football shirts in the late 1970s, its grip on the finances of clubs has become vice-like over the last thirty-odd years. Liverpool were the first top-flight English team to carry shirt sponsorship (see 'K is for Kit'), when Hitachi gained the rights to have their name emblazoned on those famous redbreasts in 1978 for the princely sum of £150,000. Fast forward to January 2014, when Liverpool announced their latest sponsor through the club's chief commercial officer. Billy Hogan hailed the arrangement after signing the multi-million-pound deal with none other than Dunkin' Donuts, the American bakery giants.

'We're delighted to be joining forces with Dunkin' Brands, one of the world's most iconic names,' he said, without any sense of irony. 'Dunkin' Donuts will be our official coffee, tea and bakery provider, and Baskin-Robbins will be our official ice cream provider – we welcome both to the LFC family.' They may not have won very much since their heyday in the 1970s and 1980s – it is twenty-five years since their last League championship and they have never won the Premier League – but at least they have secured a big, fat donut sponsorship. The fact that aforementioned Dunkin' Donuts are at the very bad end of the scale of sugary, unhealthy foods seems to have been conveniently forgotten as the LFC family gets bigger and bigger and grosser and grosser in every sense. Spare a penny, or maybe even a dime, for Bill Shankly's thoughts.

Of course, sponsorship is a key part of any club's finances, with such deals providing longer-term stability and an important source of revenue. But it is the pernicious influence that invades the corporate hospitality suites that is turning the clubs themselves into vehicles for the marketing men; that is what causes concern and threatens the soul of the game. The stadiums are becoming symbols of this new world, and the 'matchday experience' resembles going to a gig rather than a sporting event.

Paul Garred, ex-drummer of The Kooks and director and co-founder of Bootbag Media, transports us into the contemporary, sanitised world

The slick, modern turnstile with the escalator that glides you to your padded seat. Oh, the modern world is a smooth operator.

'Would you like the cottage pie or the burger with tomato chutney and gruyère, sir?' at the food kiosk.

'Is it on a seeded bap or a floured one?' I ask. Hmm, decisions. I'm wearing the new shirt of the season, but I've only bought it because I like the brand Nike. I mean, it's a template that my pub team wears, but it has the swooshy logo that makes last season's shirt by an inferior brand look like shit.

'My steak and ale pie only had ten pieces of rib eye in it,' cries one fan on the concourse. At this point, the 'mega-mix' for the kids in the family stand begins blaring 'Hey Jude' by the Beatles, because the fans can replace the name 'Jude' with the word of their beloved club. How original. But let's not look too far; the cheerleaders are synchronising a routine to the new Rihanna single. Last time I checked, I didn't realise my team came from Texas. Oh, and the star striker has just scored a cracker. The crowd go mental – it was the last minute, after all – only to be drowned out by 'Song 2' by Blur. I'm not even sure if any of Blur actually liked football, but then again, I've seen American football games on the box and they do exactly the same...

Paul's first game was a million miles from such civilisation, at the rickety Goldstone Ground to watch Palace beat Brighton 2-0 in a pre-season friendly in 1992.

As the national stadium, Wembley is at the pinnacle of the changing culture that surrounds football. Its reconstruction was a massive improvement on the old, creaking 1923 version, and was well overdue by the time it eventually took place between 2000 and 2006. Despite the massive overspend and inevitable delays, the new ground is a far more comfortable place to watch football, unimpeded by the irritating, obstructive columns and the poor line of sight many endured previously. However, the introduction of Club Wembley, or the dreaded middle tier, is one of those concessions to the corporate world that has drained the atmosphere. With just under 20 per cent of the overall capacity, Club Wembley has become a significant part of the stadium. But those 17,500 seats will, more than often not, be sparsely populated at kick-off, and for ten minutes either side of half-time. Then, of course, there is the mass exodus before full time.

The high prices, ranging from the minimum of £50,000 to secure a ten-year debenture for Gold Seats, deter the ordinary football fan – although as the promotional blurb rather charmingly points out, this works out at 'as little as £314 per event'. But enough of the cheap seats, which are a snip compared to the Bobby Moore Club seats. These will set you back an eye-watering £10,648 per annum, or £887 per event. These seem even more expensive considering the majority of Club Wembley ticket-holders only watch a maximum of sixty minutes of football, so pro rata that comes in at just shy of £900 per hour. The sight of these seats being vacated in the rush for the ice-cold chardonnay and chorizo bagels that adorn the buffet table suggests where the priorities of these punters lie. Speaking of which, I have been reliably informed that at the Emirates, another stadium that is a bastion of the corporate takeover/makeover of football, the cost of the buffet comes in at a particularly hefty £63 per head, which must mean that their Bovril and meat pies are served with a different gravy to the one usually associated with football fare.

Even the official description of Club Wembley implies a

loss of soul and spirit: a one-kilometre concourse with an array of bars, concession outlets and restaurants – there's an option to suit everyone. This feels more like one of those vast shopping centres than a football ground, where consumption and expenditure are the key features. Move over Wembley, here is Westfield. Every football fan yearns for their club to be there, but they are not expecting a dose of retail therapy into the bargain. The fact that the late Michael Jackson has had more appearances at the new Wembley than any football club indicates a shift in priorities.

When Manchester United – the self-proclaimed biggest club in the world – was recently forced to introduce a 'singing section' in order to create a better atmosphere at Old Trafford, the worm had truly turned. It is a further indication of how corporate hospitality has eaten away at the soul of football. To try to galvanise the fans into being louder is enough to make them choke on their prawn sandwiches, and Roy Keane will undoubtedly be shaking his grisly grey beard in weary admonishment.

C is for Crying

'Consider anything, only don't cry!'
Alice could not help laughing at this, even in the midst of her tears.

From *Through the Looking-Glass* by Lewis Carroll

The scene is all too familiar as the denouement of another long, hard campaign is reached; there are people in floods of tears in every corner of the stadium. The cameras search for the toughest-looking fan crying. Tattoos and tears make for such great pictures, after all. Then there are the players, who have kept everything bottled up until the moment of emotional release. Their shirts are no longer soaking up sweat, but the tears are rolling down their cheeks as it all proves too much for our battle-hardened heroes. Ten months of frustration are now spilling out for all to see.

It is all very well to be more open with our feelings, but, as sports columnist Duleep Allirajah makes abundantly clear, crying has now become a contagion that is out of control. There is a sense of vicarious pleasure in watching what used to be the preserve of the weak but has now almost become a badge of honour. Football is an emotional game, full of highs and lows, and we have all had those moments when the eyes have watered, and not just because some unfortunate soul has taken one in the knackers. I have cried mainly through relief rather than despair, when Palace escaped the drop in 2001 with Freedman's last minute goal at Stockport, and again in 2010, after surviving another relegation showdown with Sheffield Wednesday at Hillsborough.

The crying game – Duleep Allirajah

May is weeping season. It's when trophies are won or lost, when teams get promoted or relegated and, above all, it's the time when grown men cry in public. On the pitch, in the stands; it's a blubfest. And frankly, it has to stop.

It was the Geordies who introduced the world to public weeping. Gazza memorably pioneered the trend in Italy 1990. English women were supposedly converted to football in that moment. They felt his pain; their hearts were melted by a big man in tears. Gazza became an icon for a new, emotionally literate masculinity. But what was unusual in the 1990s is now commonplace. When Newcastle United fans sobbed in 1996 as their team blew the title, the lachrymal floodgates opened. The terraces were now awash with tears. The lingering, close-up camera shot of a fat bloke in tears became obligatory. While it expresses despair more articulately than Clive Tyldesley's words ever could, it feels more like grief porn than sports broadcasting.

Football, you could argue, is a passionate game. The sight of John Terry or Luis Suárez sobbing shows just how much they care. Sure, football is an emotional affair. Getting a bit dewy-eyed over your team's triumphs or tragedies is inevitable. What I find objectionable is the social value attached to emotionalism. In these therapeutic times, we're constantly peddled the line that it's good for men to cry. Go on boys, let it all out. What I hate about the canonisation of the weeping Gazza is its implicit coerciveness. The tearful footballer is an emotional role model for all of us. Men are seen as emotionally stunted knuckle-draggers who need to be taught how to express their feelings.

But why is it a good thing for grown men to weep in public? The public sphere was traditionally an arena in which emotions were expected to be kept in check, and a good thing too. We wouldn't be able to do our jobs properly if we keep bursting into tears. Even in the febrile atmosphere of a match, professional footballers need to control their emotions, to ignore the vicious backchat and crowd taunts. That fateful night in Turin, Paul Gascoigne pulled himself together. He stopped feeling sorry for himself, dried his eyes and gave everything for the team. That's the Gazza we should admire: the professional footballer, not the blubbing baby.

A fellow Palace fan, Duleep's first match was at Loftus Road in around 1970, featuring a Rodney Marsh hat-trick. He could not recall the opponents, or the final score, but he is absolutely certain that Marsh did not burst into floods of tears at the final whistle.

D is for Diving

> Diving has been in the game for years. Probably with all the coverage the game gets now, with all the cameras around, it gets highlighted a bit more. But it hasn't got any worse.
>
> Wayne Rooney in 2009

Diving is universally acknowledged as one of the, worst traits of the game. It is despicable, it is dastardly and it is damaging. However, it has become rife and there is much head shaking and hand wringing over what should be done about this particular evil that has infested the game. Regular perpetrators such as Luis Suárez are roundly castigated but remain unpunished. Retrospective action has been mooted, but it remains muted as the authorities struggle to come to terms with what they have labelled as simulation.

As far as the British are concerned, the disease that is diving is one that was originally the preserve of sneaky Europeans or dissembling South Americans. One of the most notorious cases in recent years involved a Brazilian as he was preparing to take a corner in Brazil's opening World Cup game against Turkey in 2002. The Turkish full-back helpfully kicked the ball towards Rivaldo, with a little bit of zip on it (he was no doubt trying to ensure that the ball would be placed correctly in the quadrant – see 'R is for Rules & Regulations'). But after the ball cannoned into the Brazilian's midriff, he was seen clutching his face before collapsing in a heap of pain and shame.

He did not so much go down in instalments; it was as if he were a particularly hammy actor playing the central Shakespearian hero in a five-act tragedy. So convinced by this outrageous play-acting was the referee that he brandished a second yellow card to the bemused Turkish player, and Rivaldo went down, both literally and metaphorically, in the annals of the worst cheats ever to disgrace the field of football. He became a figure of hate for besmirching the image of Brazilians as upholding the virtues of the Beautiful Game. Back in Brazil, according to Latin American football expert Fernando Duarte, there was a fair degree of consternation. The negative response was not at the principle of faking injury, but at how poor his acting skills proved to be and how silly he looked as each successive replay confirmed his melodramatic collapse.

It is a pity that some of the more gifted players like Rivaldo are also those who practice the dark arts so keenly. Their sublime skills are tainted by their propensity to make the most of any challenge to gain an advantage.

The 2014 Ballon d'Or winner Cristiano Ronaldo is arguably the greatest player of the current generation, blessed with oodles of skill and electric pace, but he does have a tendency to go down a little too easily. To make matters worse, if the referee fails to award him the free kick he has 'earned' then he pouts and postulates like a five-year-old who has had his sweet jar raided.

Ronaldo fits in with the English image that cheating and faking has blighted foreign football, but one of his former teammates at Manchester United has taken on the mantle of dastardly diving and become public enemy no.1, and he just happens to be English. Born in Stevenage, he was the archetypal Home Counties boy, who made his name playing for local club Watford. Ashley Young played schoolboy football with Lewis Hamilton, so perhaps he learned a little bit about chicanery and slippery behaviour from the young racing driver.

Young progressed to the national team after his move to Aston Villa and then moved to United in 2011, where he was seen as a possible replacement for Ronaldo, who had decamped to Madrid. Young is not in the same class of footballer, but he has certainly emulated the Portuguese winger in building a reputation for diving to such an extent that David Moyes, during his brief managerial stint, publicly criticised his antics. So endemic had Young's diving become that he was even ostracised by a large section of United fans, who were fed up with his deception. Once your own fans disown you, the message should be getting through.

It therefore appears a bit outdated and revisionist to highlight the diving disease as being solely the preserve of Johnny Foreigner, but then again, when the criticism is levelled at a Dutchman by a Frenchman maybe we should start to recognise its validity. 'Robben is very good at getting the maximum of nothing,' whinged Arsene Wenger. 'He's a great player as well as a very good diver but it's part of him.' So there you have it; according to Wenger it's in the genes, a pyrrhic victory of nature over nurture. Argument settled once and for all, by a manager who has never had a player stoop so low.

Although he may not be the most natural of bedfellows with Wenger, Tony Pulis is a kindred spirit of Arsene's on this point. Pulis took the unprecedented, but most welcome, step of fining two of his Palace players, Jerome Thomas and Marouane Chamakh, for diving in a match against Swansea. He declared, 'It's a disease. It's one we're almost rid of, but if people do it, they've got to be reminded it's not right.' That it takes a manager most closely associated with those agents of darkness, Stoke City, to hold up the beacon of truth is deliciously ironic.

Accompanying Pulis in the fight against diving disease is a player who represented a team who, like Stoke, were the antithesis of the free-flowing artistry that Wenger espouses. Former Wimbledon player Stewart Castledine makes a strong case for the prosecution over diving and, in particular, the disgraceful post-dive custom of rolling, writhing and hollering so strongly reminiscent of a spoilt toddler seeking attention. It defies physical belief to be able to roll around with such vigour, include a couple of half pikes and at the same time be seriously injured. So wrapped up in this gymnastic show of adolescence are these high rollers that they almost forget to provide their very own tour de force, the brandishing of an imaginary card – the colour of which is left to the discretion of the referee – which reminds the official of the real reason behind the amateur dramatics.

Diving – Stewart Castledine, ex Wimbledon and Wycombe Wanderers player (1991–2002), Director at James Grant

While it may not be a particularly unique hate among the football fraternity, I find it difficult to plump for anything else ahead of diving as my pet hate – particularly when it is accentuated and exacerbated by the accompanying howls of faux pain and the rolling around the turf as though the player had been shot.

To give particular context and reasoning for my personal distaste for diving, I was a playing member of the Wimbledon Crazy Gang throughout the 90s during their Premiership years.

I readily acknowledge that I was a bang average Premier League player, but I never gave less than 100 per cent, prided myself on my fitness and strength, and NEVER in my whole career went down and stayed down.

I was fortunate enough to share the dressing room with some pretty tough characters at Wimbledon, and I'd like to think that virtually all of them shared my mentality – it went a long way to ensuring we punched above our weight throughout those years.

I cannot get my head around why you would want to humiliate yourself in front of your friends, family, teammates and fans by rolling around squealing like a baby. I grew up in Twickenham and have many rugby-playing friends – the disdain and scorn that they rightly pour on us footballers is embarrassing; rugby players wouldn't dream of going down as easily as us.

It sends out a terrible message to watching youngsters that it is ok to act like a big girl's blouse if you're a footballer, and adds to the growing negative image that footballers are increasingly acquiring.

Diving is also inherently dishonest and puts the referee in an invidious position, which further undermines the player/ref relationship and makes a tough job even harder (I am also an advocate of ex-players who better understand the nuances of the game being fast-tracked into refereeing roles, which I believe would improve standards, but that rant is for another time).

To conclude, it's a contact sport and you're going to take knocks – obviously if you are genuinely badly injured then that is another matter entirely. The problem is that this increasingly worsening epidemic of diving and faking injury ensures that a 'cry wolf' scenario ensues, and no one is sure whether an injured player is actually seriously in trouble or not – if you're badly hurt then by all means get treatment, but if you're not, then man up and get on with it!

Stewart scored on his Premier League full debut at Highfield Road, Coventry 1 Wimbledon 2, on 2 April 1994. The first match he attended was First Division, Stamford Bridge, Chelsea 1 Leeds 2, on 1 October 1977.

D is for Director of Football

> Judge me on my signings.
>
> Joe Kinnear, June 2013

There cannot be many more unloved, derided job titles than the Director of Football. The very idea of having someone who hovers between the chairman and the manager is flawed, there being so little room to operate. The best-run clubs are those with a cigarette paper between the two, and anyone caught in the middle will be irrelevant at best, generally obstructive and at worst, disruptive. You can count the successful incumbents comfortably on one hand, with a few digits to spare.

When they were first introduced into British football, they were lauded as being progressive and part of a European revolution. And so that club of such great foresight, Newcastle United, appointed Dennis Wise during Keegan's second managerial reign. The choice of Wise was interesting, as Dennis' main strength as a player was his combative tenacity rather than as being one of the game's great thinkers. But Newcastle chairman Mike

Ashley was undeterred by such superficial observations, and in 2008 Wise was hired with responsibility for scouting players across the world and developing the academy. A fruitless year passed, during which many people questioned the wisdom of the appointment, and nobody shed a tear when the plug was pulled in April 2009. Wise himself summed up his tenure in not particularly glowing terms with the terse summary, 'It has all had a damaging effect on my career,' and Newcastle did not exactly rip up any trees during this period.

But Mike Ashley is not a man to be cowed into submission or allow the facts to get in the way of decisive action. So after a year or two of progress under Alan Pardew, Ashley played his trump card by appointing Joe Kinnear to be the new Director of Football. Kinnear proved to be another disaster, leaving his job less than nine months after joining, in the summer of 2013. Kinnear's record of signing not one single permanent player in the first transfer window, with only Loic Remy joining Newcastle on loan from QPR, was brushed under the carpet. The fact that Kinnear did not meet Remy until after the loan was agreed suggests he was not especially influential in that piece of business.

But when Kinnear repeated the trick in January with the solitary loan signing of Luuk de Jong, allied to the departure of their best player by a country mile, the end was nigh. When Yohan Cabaye upped sticks to Paris St Germain there were howls of dissension, which eventually led to Kinnear's resignation in February 2014. Ashley again found himself light of a Director of Football and with a growing mutinous feeling among the fans. As Kinnear asked to be judged on his signings when he took the job, there can be little doubt as to the evaluation. Whether Newcastle goes for third time lucky is open to debate, but their recent experience suggests that this is not going to bear much fruit and that it may be better for all concerned to let it lie.

E is for England

> This is a letter of hate. It is for you my countrymen, I mean those men of my country who have defiled it. The men with manic fingers leading the sightless, feeble, betrayed body of my country to its death ... damn you England.
>
> From a letter to the *Tribune* by John Osborne

One of the worst afflictions to beset any Englishman is the travail of having to follow the England team at the World Cup. Possibly the worst aspect of this regular bout of sadomasochism is the inability of the media to resist whipping us all into a frenzy in the run-up to the tournament. We do not learn the many lessons that are littered throughout history, and we allow the fantastical dream of the national team actually performing creditably to surface every four years.

Our nearest and dearest neighbours, the Scots, fell into this trap of self-delusion in 1978, when the fevered talk suggested that Ally MacLeod would be carried shoulder high through the streets of Buenos Aires by his Tartan

Army (see 'M is for Music') after securing the World Cup. As per usual, the gallant Scots did not even get out of their group, but the important thing is that our Caledonian cousins did learn their lesson from the anti-climax of that campaign and have never allowed themselves any idle fantasies of glory since.

Because of that isolated, solitary moment in 1966, the English feel emboldened to believe the hype, and steadfastly ignore all the facts surrounding their current chances. There is even the hard evidence of a book, *Why England Lose*, which explains in fine detail the inevitable conclusion. Backed with supporting arguments from the fields of economics, geography and even social exclusion, Messrs Kuper and Szymanski provide a healthy portion of realism to go along with the standard hype and the giddy notions of success.

Of course we play down the levels of expectation initially, with the vast body of journalists and pundits limiting any realistic chances. We all nod knowingly, accepting that getting out of the group phase is probably the sole objective, but once we squeeze past the might of a Trinidad and Tobago or an Ecuador then there is a mad rush for clips of that moment almost fifty years ago, and – whisper it – we might just have found form at the right time, anything can happen in the knockout phase, etc. ad infinitum.

I consider myself to be fortunate in at least being alive when England won the World Cup. I was six years old on that glorious sunlit afternoon in July 1966, when the imperious Bobby Moore led the country to its one and only international honour. Not that I remember the match particularly well, although I must have watched it; my older brother would have insisted and my parents would have indulged us.

What I do recall is going to the cinema to watch *Goal!*, the film of the tournament that followed the year after, and being struck by the glorious Technicolor nature and the sheer size of the cinematic experience. Having only seen the game on a black-and-white television set, this bright spectrum of hues was mesmeric. Here were Hurst and Peters in glorious crimson shirts, true giants bestriding the vast screen. That curiously orange ball (not sure why anyone thought it would be snowing in London in July) billowing the net as Sir Geoff finished off his hat-trick with aplomb, and Kenneth Wolstenhome's classic commentary ringing in our ears.

'Some people are on the pitch, they think it's all over [cue Hurst's third goal] ... it is now.' It was so good, it feels as though it was scripted, but it was not, and the pride of those three lions filled our chests as Moore wiped his hands dutifully and respectfully before accepting the diminutive, sparkling golden Jules Rimet trophy from the queen. That was the moment of exquisite joy, unbound pleasure, which laid the foundations for a succession of desperate disappointments that have littered the last five decades.

As an innocent, naïve six-year-old boy, I thought that this was what happened at international tournaments; it was all glory and trophies. But the 1970 World Cup shot that notion out of the water, and what was left was gory as the England team wilted in the shimmering Mexican heat. That quarter-final against West Germany was the first time I had wept over a football match (see 'C is for Crying'). Our progression to the latter stages included an honourable 1-0 defeat to Brazil, but that was viewed as a minor hiccup on the road to yet more glory.

And sure enough, we were back on track, as the old masters, Peters, Ball, Hurst and Charlton, took us into a 2-0 lead early in the second half. Even when Beckenbauer stole a goal back with twenty minutes to go by slipping one under the keeper's futile dive, there seemed nothing that could interrupt our serene passage. Indeed, just after that first German goal, Alf Ramsey decided it was time to rest Bobby Charlton from the sapping heat of Leon and save his precious legs for the semi-final.

When Uwe Seeler equalised with a looping backward header that sailed unimpeded into the far corner, there was an odd sensation that all of a sudden, things were not going according to plan. It was at this point we realised that Peter Bonetti was not Gordon Banks and that he was fallible. Extra time was painful, setting a precedent for a fear of those additional thirty minutes, which had brought glory four years earlier but which were now ready to inflict pain and torment in equal measure.

Bonetti's feebleness in allowing Gerd Müller acres of space and eons of time to volley the winning goal from inside the six-yard box was too much to bear. I hated Bonetti, as he had ruined the day, wrecked the tournament and, worst of all, messed up my ideals by destroying the illusion that England were the best. It was a cruel trick to play on an impressionable boy. And to make matters worse, it was my tenth birthday. What a way to usher in this coming of age; I entered the double-figured years with a snotty nose and red eyes.

Mr Bonetti had much to answer for with his cack-handed display that ushered the Germans into the semi-final, leaving me a blubbering, prepubescent mess. Moreover, just four days later Harold Wilson's defeat in the UK General Election was also attributed to The Cat's calamitous performance, as confirmed by Wilson's Minister of Sport Dennis Howell, who bemoaned Labour's misfortune. 'The moment goalkeeper Bonetti made his third and final hash of it on the Sunday, everything simultaneously began to go wrong for Labour for the following Thursday.' This remains the only time a government has been ousted by a goalkeeper's gaffes.

But, in retrospect, maybe dear old much-maligned Peter was doing me an enormous favour. I had experienced my first bitter taste of a disappointing England World Cup exit, showing me exactly what was to come over the next five decades. In a way, Bonetti was preparing me for the heartache and horrors that were to come. There is a distasteful and disturbing twist behind the hatred of following England at the remaining World Cup Finals. Behind the successive failures, there was the cruel exposure of the long-held myth that England had moved on from being a nation of shopkeepers to become a nation of goalkeepers. Accordingly, after the shock of 1970 had sunk in, we consoled ourselves that we may not have all the best footballers but we still were the No. 1 for No. 1s.

At least, as a country, we had that to fall back on during the dark days of the 1970s – or did we? From being invincible in 1966, we were shaken out of our superiority by 1970, and then had to face the pedestrian, demeaning task of actually qualifying for the World Cup for the first time in a dozen years. It was clearly a shock to the system, with an indifferent campaign stuttering to its denouement of a make-or-break match against Poland at Wembley.

Naturally, we backed ourselves. We were, after all, at home; we had Alf Ramsey at the helm and we had Peter Shilton, the world's finest goalkeeper. Added to which, according to the omniscient Brian Clough, they had 'a clown' called Tomaszewski as a keeper, so what could go wrong? In 1973, there were no Opta stats to keep us informed of all those vital facts and figures, such as possession or shots on and off target, but the plain truth was that England bombarded the Polish goal and the clown repelled all raiders. Then Poland had the temerity to break into our half and shoot, right under the flailing body of Shilton, who was doing a passable impression of Bonetti circa 1970. As the ball slipped under Shilton's body, so England's chances slipped into the abyss.

Not only had our invincibility been well and truly punctured, but also now one of the few facts we could rely upon – that England had the best goalkeepers in the world – was being challenged. Alf Ramsey was pushed onto his sword, a benighted knight, and to make matters worse, countries with no tradition of playing football or having decent keepers were competing in Germany – Australia, Zaire and Haiti to name but three. To cap it all off there was a team from these shores, but it was Scotland, the land of the error-prone goalie and perennial no-hopers, who had somehow supplanted England in the pecking order.

The fact that Poland were a decent team, who ended up with a highly creditable third place at the Finals, was irrelevant. How dare they not so much prick our bubble as burst it in our face and rub it hard into our mouths until we were gasping for breath. And so the litany of failure – and specifically goalkeeping failure – began to build, and with each World Cup Finals the new order was drilled home to us as expectations were systematically lowered before each tournament.

In 1978, another missed qualification, with Shilton yet again allowing a tame shot through with little resistance, meant we lost out to Italy. The only saving grace was Ally McLeod's grandiose claims that set up Scotland for a mighty fall in Argentina. They duly obliged, with a hapless, hopeless defeat to Peru and a barely imaginable goalless draw with the might of Iran, and then followed this up with a futile victory over the Dutch, who went on to the final.

Twenty years on from our last qualification, we did at long last make it to Spain in 1982 and immediately impressed with the fastest goal in World Cup history against France, which then succeeded in building up our long-forgotten view that we were top dog. And this is where we reach the real nub of this intense dislike of watching England in World Cups, and where we could have learned something from the Scots. Here is the government health warning writ loud and clear: 'Do not, under any circumstances, allow yourselves to even hint that we might be in with a chance of winning the tournament.'

The hard-luck stories are well rehearsed and trotted out to cushion the blow of failure. Take 1986, where England stumbled in the group stages, losing to Portugal and drawing with mighty Morocco, seemingly on the way home. Then Gary Lineker laid a few of those 1970s Polish ghosts to rest with a hat-trick before we pulverised plucky Paraguay, and of course fell to the Hand of God, courtesy of Diego Maradona, who out-jumped and out-punched that man Shilton. We blithely ignore the brilliance of Maradona's other goal, with our burning sense of injustice outweighing any other factor.

We tried to control ourselves in 1990, as the now typical slow start under Bobby Robson saw us draw with Ireland and Netherlands before squeaking past Egypt 1-0; suddenly it was all roses in the garden as Platt snatched the 120th-minute win against Belgium. Then the nation started to get all in a lather as we fortunately beat Cameroon, and at last, the World Cup was being restored to its rightful place. But, of course, just as we were getting comfy, along came the Germans to block our path and, despite Gascoigne's best efforts, there was the cruelty of the looping goal that left Shilton (yes, the imperious Shilton) a motionless spectator. Then there were the penalties, which our Peter did not get a sniff of as Waddle and Pearce lost their radars. This was put down to terribly bad luck and misfortune, which was now the regular accompaniment to the boys heading home early. I cried again twenty years on from those first tears, and yes, it was the Germans who inflicted the blows to deepen my desolation.

Another non-qualification in 1994 was followed in quick succession by the now familiar penalty expulsion, this time at the hands of Argentina. Although our penalty takers must accept some blame for their feebleness; when did an England keeper actually save a crucial spot kick? On to 2002 and, with solid custodian David Seaman in between the sticks, another clanger, courtesy of Ronaldinho's ridiculous shot which drifted ever so slowly over the great moustachioed one.

Back to more penalty woes against Portugal in Germany (where else?), and by the time we reached South Africa we had given up on invincibility and having the best keepers in the world, with Rob Green's horrible mistake against the USA smashing that misconception to smithereens and allowing David 'Calamity' James to come back into the fray. Here is where we turn to another key aspect of what really gets our collective goats about following our country's fortunes; it's over to Paolo Hewitt, author and writer, who shares his sorrow.

Paolo Hewitt – England on TV

The commentary. The jingoistic, casually racist outpourings which mar every game I watch. England won the World

Cup in 1966. You might have heard. They never shut up about it. Since then, there have been eleven World Cup tournaments. Eleven. And England have either not qualified or just about reached the quarter finals. And yet, listening to the practitioners of the commentary art when those Three Lions walk onto a pitch, one would assume that a major international football power was in operation, a team on level with the Brazil of the 70s, the Spanish of today, guided by a golden generation who never seem to actually … shine.

Even if England is playing appallingly, the truth is covered up. It is hilarious. I remember one game, World Cup 2010. England could not string a pass together. And then Rooney did it. He passed the ball correctly to a teammate. 'Better,' screamed the commentator, 'much, much better!' England were playing Algeria at the time.

Hewitt's first match was about as far away from the World Cup as is possible.

It was at the Kingfield Football ground in Woking, Surrey. I must have been about ten. It was a night game, and the floodlights and the atmosphere made the night very special. I had not experienced anything like it, even if it was Isthmian League level. Since then, I have always preferred floodlit football. I think the school might have taken us, because I remember sitting next to Mr Wyatt, our PE teacher, who was praising good play from players on both teams. I remember thinking that football was a strange place for such an even-handed approach, and later on, when I got to Spurs and the Mecca of Football that is White Hart Lane, I realised why.

The confirmation from FIFA that England were the thirteenth-best team out of twenty-four at the 2010 tournament did not deter the 'if only' brigade, who were soon out in force. The truth, however unpalatable it may be, is firstly that England are no longer a major force, secondly that our keepers are fallible, and lastly that none of this will affect our unerring ability to ignore all evidence and, deep down, imagine this could be the year, couldn't it?

The fact that the last words of this sorry chapter are left to Sepp Blatter sums up how much we all hate following England's World Cup adventures. To understand what depths we have fallen to, his words appear rational and well balanced. Be afraid – very afraid.

> 'As for England, ask the FA and the Anglo-Saxon world,' Blatter said. 'England is considered the motherland of football, like Brazil is considered as the deepest level of football. But ever since FIFA has existed, everybody has developed. There are no more small national teams. Perhaps there are small countries, but their national teams are strong. Football has developed everywhere. Players play in different leagues. The internationalism of football is good for some and not for others.
>
> 'One example of that is England. But it is good for Spain. All eleven starting players [in the World Cup

final] play in La Liga. All eleven. That's the difference. You can draw your own conclusions. I am trying to draw the difference between the Premier League and La Liga.'

The Guardian, 12 July 2010

F is for Footy Bores

The secret of being a bore … is to tell everything.

Voltaire, *Discours en Vers sur l'Homme,* 1737

For genuine lovers of football, it is extremely difficult for anyone to talk about the game and be boring. But there are a select few who somehow manage to do this quite effortlessly, and the members of this group are collectively known as 'footy bores'. Some people's hackles will be raised at the very sight of the word 'footy', but that is intentional. The footy bore comes in different shapes and sizes, but the uniting factor among this disparate, desperate bunch is that they go that little bit too far with their obsession and veer into territory that is extremely dangerous. For the purposes of this book, I am going to look at a couple of the main groups of footy bores so you can spot them from a distance and then studiously avoid them.

The Ground-Hoppers

Ground-hoppers are easy to detect because they will always be clearly the worst dressed person within any social gathering. Expenditure on clothes is considered trivial; indeed, any money spent outside the core activity of travelling to as many grounds as possible is branded a waste of resource. If, by any chance, you do get trapped in conversation by a ground-hopper, there is very little room for manoeuvre. It as is you have been caught in an especially sticky swamp and there is no escape.

You will be expected to be entranced by the tales of going to Exeter on a cold, wet and windy night in February, and by the detailed dissection of the away end's facilities, which will include the number of loos on offer and the variable quality of the pies available. Be prepared to revel in that wonderful moment when he finally made it to the 92 Club with that celebrated visit to Spotland, and naturally he has the badge, the tie and the annual newsletter to prove it. If said footy bore starts to retrieve the rulebook of the 92 Club to explain the finer points of membership, this is definitely time to beat a hasty retreat. Otherwise, you will be entangled in the story behind Rule 3's withdrawal and the subsequent furore that surrounded it.

Their endless enthusiasm for their hobby is admirable, as is their dedication to the cause, but it is also that singularity of purpose that renders them as undesirables. As with so many of their ilk, train-spotters, plane-spotters, etc., their loss of perspective is the most alarming trait and the one that keeps humanity a fair distance away. Ultimately it is their messianic zeal that betrays them, because they fail to comprehend how anyone could not be intrigued by the 90-degree rotation of Bournemouth's pitch or the validity of attending the MK Dons stadium.

It seems a tad cruel, and perhaps a little heartless, to pick on these hardy souls as figures of hate, but spend any length of time in their company and very soon the antipathy will build to a crescendo. Do not feel bad at leaving him on his own, because within a trice of you walking away his mind will be occupied by calculating the logistics of visiting the grounds of the next clubs to be promoted from the Conference to ensure continued membership of the 92 Club, and that smile of self-satisfaction will return.

Programme Collectors

In a similar way to ground-hoppers, programme collectors can drill down so deeply into their obscure knowledge mine that the vast majority of us get lost as the darkness envelops us. Most football fans have a random array of programmes from the past, but this casual approach to their art is anathema to the connoisseur. The minutiae of the stitching in Shrewsbury's 1980s programmes will keep aficionados entertained for days on end. Having converted the attic many years ago to house the thousands of programmes, there are far too many hours spent away from natural sunlight, classifying and then reclassifying. The crucial question that will occupy all the waking hours is whether to index alphabetically, chronologically or – in a radical departure – geographically.

Part of the lifeblood of programme collectors, or 'proggies', is the thrill of the swap. When they stumble across the guy in Morecambe who has a pristine copy of the programme from the last match at the Baseball Ground, they begin to hyperventilate. Saturday 11 May 1997, Derby *v.* Arsenal; this is it, the Holy Grail at last. The proggie has to keep calm and try to not get too excited, or else they might blow the opportunity that they have been looking for during the last fruitless dozen years. It is tough to negotiate when your heart is racing at over 1,000 beats a second and the sweat is pouring down your face in rivulets. Once secured, the programme is treated with a level of care and attention that is usually reserved for a close relative or a family pet.

Moan-Ins

The only virtue about the former groups is that they keep themselves to themselves, only rarely poking their heads over the parapets, with their public appearances few and far between. Not so with this next group, who are much more in your face and consequently more difficult to ignore. These creatures surface at around 6 p.m. at weekends, and then unleash their own brand of boredom on to the public via the likes of *606* and various other phone-ins, aka 'moan-ins'. They never miss the chance to get their oar in on a range of subjects, which can be narrowed down to either a) 'the ref was biased', or b) 'our manager should be sacked now'.

One of the main reasons that the know-it-alls are always able to air their views is that they do not have to suffer the inconvenience of actually going to watch any games. Sitting comfortably at home, they listen to the radio and/or watch the game on television and form their opinions on the received wisdom. Not that this lack of direct involvement dampens their ardour one iota; in fact, it emboldens them in their forthright opinions. So we hear that the ref was 'the worst I have ever seen', even though they were not at the match. Or 'this manager is well past his sell-by date and I won't go back until he is replaced', despite the fact that the fan in question has not been to a game for over five years. If ever challenged about their absence from the action, the riposte is usually swift and unequivocal. 'That doesn't matter; anyone can see what has gone wrong.' The stance is clear; they have made up their minds and do not need the issue to be clouded by the facts. After all, it is all about opinions, isn't it?

The Expert

The expert would never deign to get his hands soiled in the murky pools of a phone-in. This rare breed is far too cerebral to get involved in such prosaic nonsense, and is more likely to have a heated but perfectly informed debate over the development of the 'false number nine' in post-war Balkan football. Sinking to the depths of discussing anything as tawdry as the Premier League would be like asking Lord Byron to scribble down a limerick or William Walton to pen a sea shanty.

They take their bible, Jonathan Wilson's *Inverting the Pyramid*, with them wherever they travel, in search of the truth behind Ujpest Dojza's midfield trinity or the location of the first sighting of an inside left in Vienna's famed cafes. If you are ever lucky enough to be granted an audience, under no circumstances should you speak, as that would be an interjection of the most brutal and unappealing kind. All that is required is that you just nod politely and wear a smile of quiet and obedient acquiescence.

The Whinger

One of the problems about becoming a season ticket holder is the neighbours you can get stuck with. The worst of this bunch is the Whinger, whose role in life is to carp and bitch about the team from dawn to dusk. The Whinger will start when the teams are announced. 'I cannot believe he is playing after last week, did the manager not see the game ...', etc. The Whinger hardly draws breath throughout the game, unveiling a series of gestures of disapproval at every misplaced pass or lack of control. Even a goal will not satisfy him. 'Lucky the keeper dived the other way, should have put it in the corner like any half-decent striker would have done ...', etc.

Victories are treated with contempt, regarded as being extremely fortunate and thoroughly undeserved. Draws should have been victories, if only they had done the simple things correctly. Losses are vindication of the previous ninety minutes' ranting and raving, allowing full rein to the next stream of invective on the whole inept bunch. Every minute of every match is a step further into the labyrinth of despair that this sad individual occupies. The fact that you have to sit next to him throughout the season makes the whole matchday experience both unpleasant and unedifying.

The glass is not so much half full as perpetually empty, drained of the slightest enjoyment, the smallest pleasure. There is no point in addressing the issues raised, as that really sets him off on an even more virulent, impassioned attack. Whingers cannot and should not ever be challenged as this makes things a hundred times worse. So the best tactic is either to ignore, which is nigh on impossible considering the sheer volume of abuse that rolls off the tongue, or to not renew your season ticket and find somewhere else far, far away. But beware, because there are Whingers lurking everywhere and escape is not straightforward.

The Rumourmonger

Last and most certainly least are the individuals who take some perverse pleasure in circulating erroneous scores, which affect the fate of your own club. These pesky people crawl out from under their stones on the last day of the season to spread malicious gossip about what is happening elsewhere, and let's be clear; these are not mistakes or misheard information, but deliberate acts of fabrication and lies. They used to be easy to spot, as they would have a radio glued to their ear, but now, in these days of smart phones and instant access to information, they are able to blend in. But these creatures still insist on putting out false scores, which circulate around the ground, spreading like a contagion through the stands. In the worst cases, the phantom scores are transmitted to the players, who take it as a cue to celebrate prematurely and relax, safe in the knowledge that the other team has failed. They then find out, to their horror, that they have been fed a pile of porkies, but by the time the final whistle blows and the truth dawns on them it is too late to rectify the situation.

It has happened too many times to be an accident. Probably the most infamous occasion was when, in 1996, Manchester City players were under the false impression that all they had to do was avoid defeat, as relegation rivals Southampton were losing. Under the instructions of their manager, Alan Ball, having come back from 2-0 down to be drawing 2-2 against Liverpool, they started running the clock down, taking the ball into the corners and strolling happily through until the end of the game. By the time substitute Niall Quinn ran on and made the others aware that – contrary to popular belief – Southampton were actually drawing, as were Coventry and Sheffield Wednesday, City's goose was well and truly cooked.

They went down on goal difference, many fans were suspicious of Ball's Southampton connections, and no doubt the rumourmonger was skulking off into the shadows, cackling at his evildoing.

Our long-suffering Chester fan, Steve, has been at the wrong end of these ne'er-do-wells, as he recounts from the last knockings of 2013/14 season, which rendered their relegation on goal difference to be even harsher than it already was.

Tell me lies – Steve Hill

It always happens. The last day of the season, nerves shredded, and your team's survival depending on a result elsewhere. Deep into injury time it begins, a whisper to a scream, spreading like wildfire, engulfing a terrace in seconds, fingers held aloft relaying the score that will save your team. Nobody is immune; chairmen, managers and confused players are suddenly filled with belief – revitalised by news from afar.

Except it's not news. Some scrote has simply made up a rogue score for shits and giggles, briefly instilling hope before the grim realisation that nothing has changed and you're looking down the barrel of relegation. Even in an era of modern technology where you could feasibly watch the other match on your phone, it still goes on, presumably due to foul play. What kind of prick does this? The fact that they are in the stadium suggests some affiliation to the club, unless there are a series of ghouls who tour relegation-threatened clubs for their own entertainment.

Is someone at home 'having a laugh' with a fake text? Or are these phantom scores simply conjured out of thin air, fuelled by desperation? Either way, it doesn't help anyone, and we wish it would stop. Our advice: always listen to the stewards.

F is for Film

> Even the best football movies struggle to capture the sport's drama on film. The worst (and there are many) are truly abysmal.
>
> Adam Hurrey, *The Guardian*

If any self-respecting website, blog, newspaper or magazine ever needs to suddenly fill some white space, there is the hardy perennial of naming the worst football film. With so much dire material available the competition can run and run, starting with one which is a homage to the unrealistic and which has a plot that creaks so badly it is in danger of drowning out the power of Shostakovich's Leningrad, which acts as the soundtrack; *Escape to Victory* is indeed a stalwart. This 1981 film, directed by widely respected veteran John Huston, sets the benchmark as to how not to recreate a match. Even though it uses a mixture of actors and real-life footballers, none of them are at all convincing when playing football or acting, respectively. Pelé's thespian skills may be a little raw, but they are way in advance of Sylvester Stallone's goalkeeping.

There is endless fun to be had, and much space to be filled, in searching the library for the very worst screen disasters. The horror, the horror, the horror, as Brando might have put it if he had been dragged into one of these failing footy flicks. The plots do not so much creak as crack under the considerable weight of implausibility, and the 'real-life' action is about as convincing as Rivaldo's feigning in the 2002 World Cup (see 'D is for Diving'). And, lest we forget, the confluence of cinema and football was responsible for Vinnie Jones appearing alongside Stallone and Schwarzenegger in *Escape Plan*, and that is a truly unforgivable sin. The conclusion is that the only thing worse than actors trying to play football is footballers attempting to act, and never the twain shall meet. Possibly the only mixture that is more disastrous is that of football and music (see 'M is for Music'), but that is a pretty close-run contest and certainly not one to linger over, for fear of inflicting further pain and misery on those poor unfortunates who have suffered at the hands of cinematic catastrophes or musical monstrosities.

G is for Gambling

> If he (Stan Bowles) could pass a bookie's as well as he passes a football, he'd be a very rich man.
>
> Ernie Tagg, ex-Carlisle United manager

Gambling on the outcome of sporting fixtures has been going on for as long as sporting fixtures have been played. It is part of human nature to enjoy having a little punt on the horses or the outcome of a football match. Having a flutter is seen as harmless entertainment and a way of adding a tinge of excitement to our generally mundane lives. Just some harmless fun, say the advocates, and those who are against betting are viewed as puritanical killjoys. But those puritanical killjoys do have a point, as gambling has developed into a serious addiction, fed and encouraged by incessant advertising and an insatiable desire to gain a quick buck.

Just as betting has been part of the sporting scene for as long as we can remember, so has the darker, shadier side, with match-fixing scandals stretching back to the very beginnings of organised sport. Some may bemoan the lack of morality in modern times, but nefarious activities have been going for a hundred years and more. Take, for example, Stoke and Burnley, who concocted a goalless draw that suited both sides' ambitions during the 'test matches', the Victorian precursor of the modern-day play-offs, in 1898.

It has always been thus, and to rail against the concept seems antediluvian and misguided. Players are no different to general punters, apart from the fact they have much more time and much more money than Joe Public to indulge in a spot of gambling. In the days of mavericks such as Stan Bowles and the equally mischievous Charlie George, who graced (and disgraced) the game during the 1960s and 1970s, they flitted between the betting shops and fleshpots with barely a murmur. The fact that their morals were a great deal lower than their ability to entertain was considered par for the course. Their naughtiness was part and parcel of their charm, and fans were more than willing to accept the rough diamond with the smooth, silky skills; in many ways, their reputation was enhanced rather than diminished. That sense of harmless fun has been replaced by shady betting syndicates and players being accused of collusion, such as the handful charged in late 2013.

Following the very first serious betting scandal taking place in 1915, when no lesser lights than Manchester United and Liverpool fixed a match, there has been a sad litany of players taking bungs over the last 100 years. The worst case involved Jimmy Gauld, who was involved in a series of betting scandals in the early 1960s, leading to ten players being imprisoned and banned for life by the FA in 1965. Recently, high-profile players such as Keith Gillespie and Michael Chopra, and Tranmere's dismissal of their manager, Ronnie Moore, after breaching current rules, have revealed the extent of their addiction. However, despite the damage done there seemed to be little being done to counteract the problems until the FA announced a total ban on any football betting by players from the start of 2014/15 season. But gambling is now so integrated into football that one cannot imagine one without the other.

When footballers face such problems, they need support and guidance. In 2010, the chief executive of the Professional Footballers' Association, Gordon Taylor, acknowledged that there was a serious issue, declaring that there would be a 'zero tolerance' approach to gambling by players. That is all fine and good, but it has been exposed since that Taylor has been known to have the odd flutter, as his deputy Bobby Barnes revealed on BBC Radio 5 Live in September 2013, when allegations of Taylor's personal debt of more than £100,000 to a bookmaker surfaced. 'He'll have an occasional bet; it's part of society and football,' Barnes said. 'I don't think he has a problem. In his role, he's been pointing out problems for a footballer, but never said they shouldn't go out and gamble.' So much for zero tolerance.

The sheer volume of gambling on football has risen dramatically since the advent of online betting and the ubiquitous presence of Ray Winstone popping up on our screens, exhorting us in that chummy but slightly threatening manner which is at best intrusive, at worst a bit of a liberty. 'Bet 365. Bet in-play. *Now.*' Who could possibly resist such a call to arms? It is nigh on impossible to watch a match on a commercial station without being urged to have a punt. It is as if you are not getting the whole experience if you do not have a bet of some sort on the match. It is abrasive and inescapable, forever in your face imploring you to get involved.

Gambling has become the glue that sticks everything together, and its growing influence and omnipresence is taking a grip on the game, a grip that will be difficult to relinquish. For example, there is not one Premier League club that does not have either a gambling firm as a principal sponsor or an official association with a betting outfit. Where before the notion of having a small wager on your team seemed a nice idea, it has now become almost de rigueur, as a way of showing loyalty and supporting your club.

To compound matters, there is a continuous stream of people on Twitter who somehow have decided that it is fascinating to look at their own betting slips and marvel at the brilliance of their selections. So now we can all revel in the fact that Port Vale winning away completed their accumulator for £95.60. How very impressive. Quite why we are supposed to be doing cartwheels because someone has a successful bet is beyond me. With the barrage of messages, advertisements and sponsorships continuously thrust in our faces morning, noon and night it is almost impossible to avoid, so you might as well join in. After all, it is just harmless fun.

G is for Gloves

> 23.1 The outfield players may wear gloves. The gloves shall be an Equipment item separate from the shirt.
>
> From FIFA's Equipment Regulations

The sight of players wearing gloves is one of those things that really gets the blood boiling, especially when the transgressors persist in doing so in late March. It may be just about acceptable when playing in Moscow in sub-zero temperatures, but really, springtime in the UK does not remotely justify additional clothing, including glove wearing. After all, the players are meant to be running around a bit, and the chances of frostbite are greatly reduced if you are involved in physical exercise. One of the first exponents was John Barnes in the 1980s, who freely admitted that he could not stand the cold as his Jamaican roots were chilled to the bone. Barnes was also an advocate of tights, but he was not the trailblazer on this front.

The donning of ridiculous extraneous clothing can be put down to the late Leicester City legend Keith Weller, who in January 1979 broke not only with tradition but also many people's faith in footballers when he wore tights against Norwich in an FA Cup tie. Not only did Weller wear tights, but he wore white, glossy ones, no doubt aiming to emulate the whiteness of the boots of trendsetters Ball and Hinton (see 'Y is for Yellow Boots'). It just did not look right or feel right. Thankfully, nobody followed suit, and Weller's unique contribution remained very much a one-off.

The unsubstantiated rumour was that Weller first used a pair of his wife's tights, to test the practicality of wearing them while playing, before going on to pioneer those natty white ones. This may constitute the breakthrough for cross-dressing in football and opened up a massive can of worms that has developed into all manner of items, including leg warmers, mittens and even the dreaded snoods. These were derided by that good old-fashioned centre forward, Tony Cascarino:

> It's like a fashion accessory, and personally, I think it's typical of the modern footballer. I don't want to seem like a dinosaur, but I think the modern game is full of players who are of the 'softer option' when it comes to playing football. I would see it as a weakness, slightly, that they're not a real man.

But Tony would do well to consider that there was a precedent set by Weller and his white tights some thirty years before the snood reared its head.

It is dangerous to speculate quite where we are heading with this, but it conjures up images of more and more clothing being donned until we reach the nadir of when the first onesie might be worn on the pitch. And if that is not a warning to all those wearing gloves on an April afternoon I do not know what is. The unspeakable trauma of this nightmare future may have Keith Weller spinning in his grave, but he is partly culpable, for having broken rank with his one-man white tights revolution.

H is for Haircuts

> One of the causes, by the way, of the apparent lack, at the present time, of great men lies in the poverty of the contemporary male coiffure.
>
> From *Complete Essays* by Aldous Huxley, 1920–25

There is nothing that defines our appearance more than our haircut. We can chop and change clothes to suit the mood, but our coiffure is a signature that stays with us for a while. It is often said that footballers have too much time on their hands, and to fill in the boring bits in between training, playing matches and other nefarious activities (see 'G is for Gambling'), they often allow their imaginations to run wild and come up with a crazy haircut. Such is the tendency to have the wackiest style that there are books dedicated to the subject, and so spoilt for choice is anyone compiling these tomes and picking out suitable targets that it is like shooting fish in a barrel.

Jason Lee will be forever remembered, not as a rampaging centre forward who graced the Premier League with Forest or won the Second Division championship with Watford, but simply as 'Pineapple Head'. Lee's choice of hairstyle became the talking point of the terraces. Thanks to David Baddiel and Frank Skinner's campaign on the Fantasy Football League programme, Lee's hair drew much more attention than his goal scoring prowess. The ridicule was heaped high, and to such an extent that Lee complained his self-confidence had been shot to pieces, or pineapple chunks perhaps. Lee decided enough was enough, had his locks shorn and tried to put his pineapple moniker behind him. But, like Samson, he was never quite the same player, and he drifted across the lower leagues with a host of clubs, still in search of his mojo.

While Lee was recognised for his singular, distinctive style, there are other players who have adopted such a vast range of different approaches to their hair that the pre-match tension will be focused on what the player's head is going to display this week. Djibril Cisse and El Hadji Diouf were two such players who experimented endlessly with ever more ridiculous and outlandish ideas. To add to the mix there were differing colours, styles and even words shaved into the side of Cisse's bonce. Perhaps his most fetching effort was the green strip on the top of his head that looked like a stray sod of turf, or maybe the spider's web he sported at Auxerre. It is a wonder that either Cisse or Djouf managed to fit any training in around the crucial task of, firstly, thinking up the next cut, and, secondly, executing their choice. Some Liverpool fans might argue that both players appeared to have put more effort into

2. Djibril Cisse sported more haircuts than goals. Here is his spider-web style, which was as close to the net as he came during his career with Liverpool, Sunderland *et al.*

their looks than honing their goal scoring skills.

This affliction for sporting natty dreadlocks even affected the style icon that is David Beckham, who managed to make a mockery of his reputation as a fashion leader when he unforgivably opted for cornrows. What possessed him to imagine that having a head that resembled a badly cut field of barley was a good idea is hard to fathom, but to be fair to him he did then shave all his hair off in an act of penance for this great crime against humanity, and has clearly not looked back since.

When it comes to style there are not many nationalities that lead the way more convincingly than the Italians. From early Roman times through the Renaissance and all the way up to the present day, Italians have been at the forefront of fashion and looks. They are also pretty good at football, and so the confluence of these two factors has led to some very good-looking players, such as Paolo Maldini, Roberto Mancini and Andrea Pirlo, allied with endless supplies of skill.

Among the greats stands Roberto Baggio, whose elegance and innate sense of balance was topped off by his hair, and who rightly earned the moniker of 'The Divine Ponytail'. Roberto managed to combine his Buddhist faith with an unusual haircut, but still managed to look cool. Unfortunately he also inspired others to emulate him, and a succession of fashion failures, including goalkeepers David Seaman and Julian Speroni, followed in his wake.

When Speroni first arrived at Crystal Palace in 2004

he sported a ponytail, attracting much attention from the fans. They dedicated a little ditty to the Argentinean, to the tune of an appropriately Italian song, 'Volare', as made famous by Dean Martin:

> Speroni wooa Speroni woooa.
> He's got a shit haircut
> He's gonna keep us up.

It was indeed a shit haircut, but unfortunately he did not succeed in keeping them up. Once Speroni had settled in London, he very sensibly returned to a much more modest short back and sides. The song is now a distant memory, and ten years on Jules is still plying his trade in SE25, having become a firm fan favourite and been voted the club's Player of the Year for the fourth time in 2014.

As for David Seaman, he did not have the excuse of either moving to a new city or not understanding the language; nor yet did he have the folly of youth to hide behind when he developed his penchant for the ponytail. It was very much in evidence during the 2002 World Cup (see 'E is for England'), when that infamous Ronaldinho hoof sailed over David's luxuriant mop of hair and ended up in the England net. Maybe it was the distraction of having this new hairdo that ultimately put paid to England's chances during that ill-fated quarter-final in Shizuoka. Not so much the divine ponytail as the bovine one.

Talking of World Cups, there is a stain on the history of

the globe's greatest sporting tournament that will never be erased. It happened back in 1998, but it still brings back shudders of apprehension as if it were yesterday. This is one of the blackest marks of all twenty World Cups, across the eighty years of its existence. When the Romanian team decided en masse to have a blonde rinse as part of their pre-match preparation, everyone was aghast. It was not just that they looked like a sub-standard boy band, nor that they stood out like a collection of sore thumbs. It was the very notion that this was a good idea that chills the blood. It was inexcusable, it was horrendous, and it was something that the Romanian nation will never be able to live down. The fact that this Romanian team, with the likes of Hagi, Dumitrescu and Petrescu, were a talented bunch made it all the worse, and provided the very blackest (or blondest) of episodes.

H is for Hatred

> Love, friendship, respect do not unite people as much as common hatred for something.
>
> From *Notebook* by Anton Chekhov

There is an unwritten but cardinal rule in supporting a club that demands the utmost rivalry, not just plain enmity but pure, unadulterated vitriol from both sides of the divide. There is a compulsion that forces the fans to loathe and abhor the enemy with no quarter given. Having grown up in Glasgow and played for clubs in London and Liverpool, Pat Nevin knows all about such rivalry and explains his own antipathy towards such tribalism. However hard he tried to avoid it, hatred followed him wherever he played or watched football. Nevin, a former Chelsea, Everton and Scottish international, is now a writer and broadcaster. He supports Hibernian, Chelsea and Everton (in no particular order).

Pat Nevin on Hatred

Fortunately, I've always loved football, particularly the playing part, but watching it is great fun too. Finding something I hate about it is more difficult. I come close to hating diving and cheating, but then realise that it is the ultimate responsibility of the governing authorities to stamp it out. Retrospective bans from reviewed video evidence would sort it out in a jiffy, but football is still run by a myopic bunch of Luddites. They will get there eventually.

I am not keen on the game's celebrity culture, the arrogance of its wealth and the self-indulgent indifference of some players who are uninterested in the true fans that spend every available penny they can afford, and sometimes that they cannot afford, following them. Still, it isn't quite hatred, just extreme disappointment.

So what do I hate? Easy. I hate the hatred that seethes within the ranks of some supporters. I used to support Celtic, and was expected to hate Rangers. I didn't. I despaired of the religious apartheid Rangers practiced but when they finally signed a 'Catholic' player, they were just another team. Many years later I changed to following Hibernian, partly to get away from the excessive tribalism inherent in the 'Old Firm' dynamic, but even in Edinburgh I was expected to suddenly hate Hearts, the Hibees' main rivals. I'm sorry, but I just don't. Actually, scrub that, I am not sorry.

Trying to explain to some people that you can support your team passionately without hating your rivals and their fans is beyond their understanding. To those people, it is clear that obviously I don't care enough, or I am not a 'real' supporter, or I am lying and I actually do hate the opposition really, or even that I am turning my back on my heritage by refusing to hate. Each of these has been suggested, along with the accusation that my stance is there only to smooth my passage as a broadcaster.

From the other side, opposition fans to the teams I support (Hibs, Chelsea and Everton) tell me that they have heard me say that I hate their team, which is nonsense. If at any time I am critical technically or tactically of their side when following my current profession as a pundit, they claim it is nothing but plain bias and barely hidden hatred, of them and of their club. This occurs even when there is a perfectly reasoned argument explaining their teams' deficiencies, which, after all, is the job.

I have come to the conclusion that those who define themselves not only by the love of their own team but by the level of hatred they have for their rivals, will never understand those of us who are not driven by animosity, but driven purely by the positive love of the team and indeed the game.

Maybe the hatred is not as prevalent as it currently appears to be – Twitter is after all a very twisted vision of modern society – but it is out there, and it can be bitter, vengeful and sometimes dangerous. So, to be clear, I do not hate football fans who are hateful; I just hate their hatred.

Nevin's first match as a player was Clyde *v.* Cowdenbeath on 7 November 1981; the first match he attended was Celtic *v.* Dunfermline in the late 1960s.

The sheer vitriol, stoked by the religious divide that engulfs the Old Firm matches, is alarming. But for some unknown reason fellow fans do not shun such brutal tribalism; they actively seek to recreate it, and so we have a string of copycat rivalries. Dundee United and Aberdeen followed in the wake of their Glaswegian rivals with the New Firm. And even in sleepy, rural East Anglia they have their very own version with the Old Farm derby. This all goes to show that if you have not got someone to hate then you are not a 'real' fan.

My own club, Crystal Palace, have indulged in this practice by developing a fierce rivalry with Brighton & Hove Albion that goes back to the days of Alan Mullery and a few seasons of parallel ups and downs for both clubs during the late 1970s and 1980s. This is despite the fact that we have much closer teams, geographically, such as Charlton and Millwall. But as nobody likes Millwall and they do not seem to care, there is not much mileage in that one, and as for Charlton, they hate us much more than we hate them as they shared our ground for a few years and bitterly resented our magnanimous gesture. The fact that there is almost forty miles between the respective grounds does not dilute the animosity, and the A23 derby is among the fiercest I have witnessed, even though a neutral is dumbfounded by its very existence.

The ridiculous nature of how rivalry affects fans can be summed up when that bitter rival is playing a team that is a direct challenge to your own team's prospects. Half of you wants the challenger to fall because it will improve the position of your club, but the other half pines for 'the enemy' to lose, and so you get caught in the trap of enmity. There are no winners and no losers, just a very confused supporter hovering between the devil and the deep blue sea, hoisted by his own petard.

That such dedication to hatred often gets in the way of positive support is of no concern to those who indulge in it. Considering Pat Nevin's illuminating contribution, it is ironic that it is the Scots who probably suffer more than any other from this syndrome, whether it is the acrimony of the Glaswegian divide or the support of any national team against England. The passion shown and the energy expended in antipathy will often outweigh the support of their own cause, and undermines the success of their own team. Leave carping about the England team to the English. We are past masters at it (see 'E is for England').

I is for Interviews

> A quotation is what a speaker wants to say – unlike a sound bite, which is all that an interviewer allows you to say.
>
> Tony Benn in a letter to Anthony Jay, August 1969

In the heat of battle, many loose and unconsidered words are uttered. The same can hardly be said for post-match interviews; even though there has been time to chew on what has just happened, there are rarely any words of much interest or insight. One of the key reasons for the banality of the answers is that the same questions are rolled out with monotonous regularity, allowing such little room for anything noteworthy. Added to this, there are always the club press and publicity officers, carefully guiding the questioners away from the nitty-gritty and towards the anodyne and anaemic. As Clarke Carlisle, former player and PFA chairman and now pundit and summariser for ITV and BT Sport, points out, if you ask a dumb question you will get a dumb answer.

Clarke Carlisle on exclusive interviews

There is no duller part of the whole industry than 'the exclusive interview'. It amazes me that after some three decades of these 'cut and paste' questions with equally predictable answers, we still endure the weekly rigmarole. How many times will a manager be asked, 'Are you expecting a response from your side today?' because they lost the week before? Or whether they'll 'be looking to maintain your momentum?' after a prior victory? When will we actually open our eyes to the fact that players will *never* tell the truth when asked, 'What do you think of the new manager?'

Football is a self-preservation society. Honesty is something that is rarely proffered, as it will likely be held against you, either in the form of an FA charge or a club fine. Ultimately, I don't believe that the media or supporters want the truth anyway, because, when confronted with a character who does speak their mind, that character is viewed as egotistical, mocked for their inferior talents or simply labelled stupid. See Joey Barton, Ian Holloway and Jack Wilshere as prime examples.

Carlisle's professional debut was for Blackpool away at Wrexham on 2 September 1997.

Carlisle is right in pointing out that interviewees rarely veer away from the straight and narrow for fear of being disciplined. In a similar vein, the publicity machines of the clubs control so many press conferences that neither managers nor players will offer an independent opinion.

With their public relations man in close attendance and ready to swoop to intercept any tricky questions like Franco Baresi in his prime, the manager or the player is hidebound by convention, and if they stray off-message they are quickly hauled back into line. This is why any unguarded, outspoken comments are treated like gold dust by the media.

Kevin Keegan's spontaneous combustion during the 1996 Premiership title run-in, when he blasted Alex Ferguson's suggestion that Leeds would not be trying that hard against Keegan's Newcastle side, is well remembered because of its rarity. To hear the genuine feelings of anyone in the game, but particularly a manager, expressing such scorn for his rival in such an open and, dare we say it, refreshing manner, was a revelation. Considering the thousands of interviews that are conducted over the course of a season, the fact that this one incident from almost twenty years ago was so memorable indicates the paucity of entertaining or enlightening ones.

One of the most irritating aspects of the interviewing process and the entire media circus that has built up around football is the constant banging of the drum that this is a communications business, when the last thing that happens is genuine communication. The clearest example of this is the false use of interpreters, by managers in particular. Tottenham's new manager, Mauricio Pochettino, never speaks without the use of an interpreter, although he revealed in late 2013 that he can speak perfectly good English. The Argentine explained that he uses the interpreter as 'he gives me the security that

... nothing is misconstrued'. Or alternatively, everything can be construed in favour of the club, with any comment that strays from the party line being expunged or replaced by the middleman. George Orwell would have had an absolute field day portraying such control thirty years on from his eponymous novel.

Alongside the screening done by interpreters, there is also the galling custom developed by players of having their massive headphones attached almost hermetically to their ears while being interviewed. Such a practice smacks of an attitude that says, loud and clear, 'You may ask me questions but I am not that interested and would rather be listening to some tunes, thanks all the same.' It is not as if footballers have particularly good taste in music (see 'M is for Music'), or that they do not have enough free time to indulge in their favourite beats. Just take the phones off for a few minutes. It won't kill you, and you might be able to communicate a little more easily.

When the interviewer finally does squeeze out some words of wisdom from the reluctant, truculent protagonist, the result is not particularly noteworthy. Back to Steve, the Chester fan, who captures the scene with searing accuracy:

> 'Interviewer: You scored all nine goals against your bitter rivals; three of them overhead kicks from your own half. How did that feel?
> Player: The main thing is the team got three points.'
>
> Just – the whole media-trained pointlessness of it.

Considering how bland and anodyne the vast majority of interviews are, it is amazing what a kerfuffle is caused if anyone has the temerity to pull out of an interview. Witness the righteous indignation when Arsene Wenger refused to speak to the assembled ranks of the press in the wake of his nightmarish 1,000th match in charge of Arsenal. One could hardly blame him for avoiding the poisonous barbs that were being readied to be fired his way in light of the 6-0 drubbing by Chelsea. It is difficult to imagine how he could have responded with any grace or dignity after that horrendous shellacking at the hands of his nemesis, Jose Mourinho. You can bet your bottom dollar that one of the first questions lined up would have been along the lines of, 'How would you rate this humiliation on the scale of failure that you have endured over the last nine years, Arsene?'

Managers are compelled to face the media, but more often than not we are left nonplussed and none the wiser. Wenger's dodging of that particular bullet would have attracted a fine, as there is a stipulation that managers have to conduct post-match interviews regardless of the circumstances, but that would have been a financial penalty worth paying for Wenger. The pain and degradation is portrayed in front of the media, and this can make for extremely uncomfortable but compelling viewing. It is akin to the sort of grilling that heads of Japanese companies are subjected to when things have gone wrong and they are forced to face the public. There is no hiding place, and it feels as though this ritual humiliation is part of the penance that has to be paid for past transgressions.

This practice seems as cruel as it is unnecessary; we will not learn anything from what has become a modern form of bear-baiting.

Of course the most famous example of the 'non-interview' was Sir Alex Ferguson's boycott of the BBC in response to a perceived slight on his son Jason in a 2004 television documentary. This was no ordinary silence but a long, protracted ban that went on for seven years. It left a void in their coverage, as Manchester United were the dominant force in English football, but Ferguson was adamant. Instead, we had to put up with various unwilling assistants such as Mike Phelan, who were dragged into view, blinking nervously at this sudden attack of the limelight. During his self-imposed exile, Ferguson did have time to fire a shot at his own *bête noire*. 'I think the BBC is the kind of company that never apologise and they never will apologise. They are arrogant beyond belief.' Ferguson's attack was perhaps the most interesting thing that was said during the long-running feud, and certainly of greater significance than most other post-match exchanges. The irony is that this pearl should come during the longest impasse between a leading manager and the national broadcaster.

Ferguson did deign to be interviewed again in 2011, but only after Mark Thompson, the Director General, brokered a peace deal in person. This was on the principle that if the Glaswegian is not going to make his way over to the mountain then the mountain has to make tracks towards him. But, understandably, there was hardly any serious line of questioning, as journalists steered clear of upsetting the irascible Scot for fear of inciting another boycott. So anyone expecting searing insight or tactical revelations should start looking elsewhere for any germs of truth or pearls of wisdom.

Alongside the stream of pointless post-match interviews and, in a way, acknowledging their futility, there is now the in-depth television interview. This is usually publicised as being frank, honest and candid, thus setting it apart from the standard ones. The main feature of these revelatory pieces is that they are shot in semi-darkness, as if it somehow adds some gravitas to proceedings. Everything is a little moody and atmospheric, but the result is that the interviewee comes across as if they were some shady underworld character confessing to past misdemeanours. 'Back in the nineties we did lose a couple of players, but the less said about that, the better,' etc. In the end, there is very little to distinguish these searching insights from the inane interviews on offer elsewhere.

J is for Joy

> On with the dance! Let joy be unconfined;
> No sleep till morn, when Youth and Pleasure meet
> To chase the glowing Hours with flying feet.
> From 'Childe Harolde's Pilgrimage' by Lord Byron

Football has inspired many joyous moments. The thrill of unbridled pleasure as the result of a late goal or over a crucial victory is one of the strongest, purest emotions that fans can experience. It is therefore a pity that such elation has been sullied by some players, when they bring out their overly orchestrated celebrations. These are not spontaneous outpourings of delight, but they are premeditated, contrived, and quite often deeply embarrassing to one and all. They make a mockery of the simple pleasures that football can bring, and there is no justification for their elaborate artificiality. There should no place for them on a football field but they are alarmingly common.

Some of the worst examples of such undignified behaviour involve players who have a point to prove, and who view the scoring of a goal as a means of showing off their plumage in some sort of narcissistic orgy. Fair enough, goalscoring is the aim of the game, but it is not all about the individual. The various protestations scream out, 'Look at me, look at me.' The subtext is: forget about the team, as they are not important right now, and just focus all your attention on little old me. Among the most frequent aberrations is the art of pointing to the name on the back of the shirt as if to say, 'In case you forgot, I am the man.' And this preening is, more often than not, directed at the manager who might have had the temerity to have dropped the player or questioned his ability in the past.

One of the worst exponents of this 'love me' brigade was Argentine Facundo Sava, who played for Fulham a couple of dozen times in a brief spell between 2002 and 2004. Facundo's party trick was to rummage inside his sock and whip out a mask, which he then slipped casually on to his face, as if it was the most natural thing in the world to do. Thankfully Sava only notched six times so we were spared overuse of his laughable Zorro impression. The fact that the mask that he so carefully placed in his sock every match went unused over twenty times was a blessing in disguise.

A much more physical manifestation of the art of self-love came from the tragicomic figure of Shefki Kuqi. He mastered a dive that was not particularly swallow-like, being more akin to the fat kid's belly flop in the local swimming baths. The Finn would set off to find a safe landing place and then launch his not inconsiderable frame into the air and land splayed out on the turf. His unique and vaguely masochistic brand of goal celebration must have made him the bane of groundsmen across the land; they would have had to repair their precious pitches from the impact of the 'Flying Finn', particularly towards the end of his career, when his weight started to attract almost as much attention as his celebrations.

One of the few rule changes (see 'R is for Rules & Regulations') that we can all endorse is that of booking a player for over-the-top displays when the boundaries of common decency and decorum are transgressed. One of the most common ways of doing this is by removing the shirt to reveal an undershirt with a preordained message. When used to highlight a noble cause, this is acceptable, such as Robbie Fowler's support for a group of sacked dockworkers, but when it is merely another way of a player blowing his own trumpet then it is neither big nor clever. The other side of Fowler's character was shown with his goal-line snorting effort in the Merseyside derby in April 1999.

The dishonour of being the king of the egotists must lay firmly at the door of Mario Balotelli, whose errant ways were most memorably commemorated when he scored in Manchester City's 6-1 demolition of Manchester United in October 2011 and revealed his fetching 'Why always me?' t-shirt, with the arrogance and chutzpah that had become his trademark during his brief and tempestuous stay in Manchester. Balotelli's routine after scoring was to stand stock-still and pose with a distinct absence of any pleasure or joy. Football is often described as a circus, and Mario became the ringmaster.

However, the most reprehensible of all is a series of generic celebrations that are designed to wind up the fans and which stain the characters of the perpetrators to such an extent that each of the players is branded forever. The first of these distasteful gestures is the cupping of the ear to opposition fans; not the worst by any means, but still highly irritating and inflammatory. Next up, or down in terms of morality, we have the 'shhh' sign with fingers pressed to the lips, inviting the fans, not so politely, to shut up.

The very worst, the very lowest of the low, revolves around those players who insist on showing off their allegiance to their current club at the moment they have just scored against one of their former clubs (see 'X is for Ex-Factor'). This involves kissing the badge, rather too ostentatiously and with a little too much relish, in the faces of those who once idolised them. This practice is the football equivalent of stabbing someone in the heart and then twisting the knife again and again to inflict the deepest possible psychological damage.

The prime example, and one which still rankles, is Ian Wright on the very last day of the first Premier League season. He had already come back to haunt Palace once with the winning goal at Selhurst in November 1992, but the true comeuppance was not to be delivered until the last match of the season at Highbury. Wright showed a massive display of his lifelong, undying affection for the Gooners after he had scored the first of the three goals that condemned Palace to an unlikely and heartbreaking relegation; forty-nine points was not enough, and we went down after Oldham somehow won their last three games, relegated by a goal difference of just two (Ian Wright) goals.

This was how he showed his gratitude to the club that had plucked him out of obscurity and, in the process, turned a non-league footballer into an England international. So thanks, Wrighty. Your overzealous enjoyment will always stick in Palace fans' craws. No doubt on his way home he drowned a couple of cute, cuddly kittens and ran over the odd panda just to confirm his status as the worst person in Christendom.

Some would argue that the very opposite of lauding a goal against a former club is a sin, and that it does not get much worse than the very deliberate 'non-celebration'. This is meant to be a sign of respect for erstwhile employers, colleagues and fans, but it can stir up as much fury as a full on, in-your-face jig. Many of us have grown sick and tired of the supposedly altruistic gesture, and challenge the genuine motivation that lurks behind the lack of any enjoyment of putting one over one's old team.

One of the first and still the most well-known 'non-celebration' came in a 1974 Manchester derby at the end of the season. Denis Law's apologetic demeanour after he scored for Manchester City at Old Trafford in the very last minute was born out of a heartfelt disappointment at hurting his old club. Although the back-heeled goal was not the decisive factor in relegating United, it felt like a hammer blow, and Law was not one to dance on the grave of the team he had served so well over eleven years. His fellow City players tried to raise some element of pleasure in this feat, but after surrounding and cajoling him to express some pleasure they could not even coax a smile out of the disconsolate Scot. The goal sparked a mass pitch invasion by long-haired, flare-trousered fans, and the game was called off shortly afterwards. As the other players trooped off the pitch, Law could be seen leaving the stage with regret writ large across his forehead, untouched by fans, who understood and appreciated the lack of any satisfaction on his part.

But what Law did forty years ago bears little resemblance to some of the cant and hypocrisy seen since. Genuine contrition is acceptable, laudable even, but when a player goes down this road after scoring against a club he once spent a few months on loan to three years ago, the validity has to be questioned. The motivation is not clear, and it seems as though this is more to do with the new norm rather than any deeper feeling for the club in question. As scoring against former clubs is almost par for the course, the whole thing has become a little wearisome. It rankles, because if the player does feel a stronger affinity with his old club, what does that say about the relationship with his current club? It suggests that somehow the dim, distant past is much more important than the here and now.

Last, and probably least, is the deeply troubling military salute. The origins or the source of the military salute celebration are a little shady, and understandably so, as it appears so incongruous when used on a football field. Emmanuel Adebayor has become a prime exponent, but

3. Tim Sherwood and Chris Ramsey dutifully return Emmanuel Adebayor's salute, a few weeks before Sherwood was sacked after only six months in charge of Tottenham.

we have not had any clear explanation as to why, or the significance. The mirroring of the salute by his manager and coaching staff just compounds the problem. When Tim Sherwood and Les Ferdinand stand to attention there is a little part of us that shrivels and dies; it just feels plain wrong, somehow, especially considering Adebayor's horrific experiences with the attack on the Togo bus in Angola in 2010 during the African Nations Cup. Maybe, considering Sherwood's imminent departure, it was akin to the White Hart Lane firing squad, but it is bizarre.

Ronaldo has also used something along similar lines while playing for Real Madrid, but that was a specific barb aimed at everyone's favourite FIFA official, Sepp Blatter, after he had made a derogatory remark about Ronaldo in comparison to his rival Messi. Describing the Portuguese star as 'a commander on the pitch' as opposed to the Argentine's 'good boy' image, Blatter provoked an inevitable response, with Ronaldo's army gesture cocking a snook at Blatter's inflammatory comments. Maybe, when the spectre of Qatar 2022 comes ever closer, a mopping of the brow celebration might be in order to highlight the absurdity of Sepp and his cronies awarding the World Cup to such an undeserving cause.

K is for Kit

Beware of all enterprises that require new clothes.

From *Walden* by Henry David Thoreau

The strength of the emotional bond that is engendered by the team's choice of kit should never be underestimated. Look at the furore whipped up by Cardiff's Malaysian owner, the infamous and infernal Vincent Tan, insisting on changing the Bluebirds' shirts to red. It was an action that served as an appropriately coloured rag to a bull for most supporters. Typical of the shock engendered by Tan's trampling of tradition and ditching of the blue shirts was the reaction of *Urban75* editor Mike Slocombe, who cried foul at the Malaysian's manipulations.

> I thought nothing would ever sway me from supporting my club until the arrival of the billionaire megalomaniac Vincent Tan, who swiftly embarked on a campaign of jettisoning all the things I loved about my team. The strip changed and the badge was replaced, as the club's proud

> history and heritage was stripped clean in a quest for transnational commercial success.

Indeed, so incensed was Slocombe that he turned his back on a lifetime of supporting Cardiff and adopted a non-league club instead. Slocombe sums up his frustration at this toying with the fans' affections, and explains his switch of allegiance from South Wales to South London.

> Most of all, I don't want to play any part in Vincent Tan's rebranding of the team that I've supported all my life.
>
> So I've moved on to the joys of non-league football, a place where fans matter and self-expression hasn't been legislated out of the ground. I now support Dulwich Hamlet FC (I live in south London and can walk to their ground).

The message is loud, and piercingly clear. Fans can put up with all sorts of remodelling, rebranding, moving to new grounds and a host of radical changes – all of which will test their loyalty – but woe betide anyone changing the team's kit, because that is certainly the last straw for camels, bluebirds, tigers, etc.

There have been some truly ghastly eyesores in the past and there was a particularly gruesome period in the late 1980s and early 1990s, when experimenting with designs was allowed to run unchecked by taste or rational thought. Step forward Hull City for their 'tiger print' abomination, launched for the 1992/93 season.

This was quite rightly voted as the worst kit of all time and it screams 'run away' at you, even in black and white.

The technicoloured horrors of previous decades have thankfully been buried for a while now, but there are still some crimes against fashion knocking around. Barcelona's away kit for 2012/13 became known as the 'Tequila Sunrise' special, but not in a good way. The launch of a new kit can spark more controversy than the signing of a new player, and the media feeding frenzy which follows will often escalate to extraordinary heights as fans are expected to shell out for the third European away in violet diagonal stripes with purple shorts and canary yellow socks. As kits change with the wind, the one permanent

4 .

Even in glorious black and white, this Hull shirt from 1992/93 season oozes horror. Just consider yourself lucky this was not in colour.

feature is that fashion will have fled over the hills many years ago, leaving shirt design in its wake.

Comedian, writer and presenter Kevin Day is under no illusions as to how bad things have become. In a country known for its catwalks and haute couture, there lurks a fashion faux pas that puts everything else into the shade.

Kevin Day on French football shorts

But my real hatred, my passionate hatred, is for the most heinous crime in international football. Not the fact that Diego Maradona still isn't in prison for stealing the World Cup. French football shorts. They've calmed down a bit lately (the shorts, not the French), but there was a time when it looked like Jackson Pollock had landed himself a job at Nike.

Firstly, they seem to have colours in France that even Timmy Mallet in his pomp would have baulked at wearing. How many shades of yellow are there? The Tour de France seems to have settled for one. French football teams are still experimenting and won't rest until they reach three figures.

Secondly, I don't know what or who Cerise is, but I'm damn certain it, or she, shouldn't be included in the description of a football team's shorts.

Thirdly, I could live with the colours if they were unadorned, but French football allows advertising and sponsor names on shorts as well as shirts. I'd like to be able to report that most French teams have either declined that option or allowed themselves a subtle, well-positioned bit of product placement that didn't sully the fine history of their football club. Instead, they mostly opted for the sort of garish publicity-seeking that is so blatant even girls in Amsterdam shop windows have been known to say, 'Oh, steady on.'

Football kits, like football, should be plain and unadorned. I hate anything else. And that's just one of the reasons I love football.

According to his father, Kevin's first match was at Selhurst Park, on the opening day of 1969/70 season, against Manchester United. Kevin's own memory is of April 1971, when Palace beat Stoke 3-2.

Paul Kelso, Sky Sports football correspondent, has similar views to Kevin Day, but he is even more specific in his distaste, focussing not just on the kit and its many awful manifestations but on the launch of said kit where all the hype is not necessarily reflected in the enthusiasm of the reluctant, recalcitrant models.

Paul Kelso – The kit launch

Ignoring, for the moment, the need for fundamental structural reform to preserve the soul of English football, I'll settle for a minor side effect of the rampant commercialism that has infected the game: kit launches.

It's not the kits per se. After three decades of sartorial abuse, no combination of colour or pattern has the power to shock. Swansea away in aubergine & primrose? Villa in hi-vis green? Whatever.

Nor is it the scandalous frequency with which they change, and I'm also ignoring the gratuitous wearing of second kits for no good reason. (The ONLY reason to wear a change kit – note, it's called a change kit, not an 'away' kit to be worn when playing away from home as a matter of course – is a genuine colour clash. Tough if you work in the Norwich commercial department, but Delia should have thought of that.)

No, the aspect of the whole kit caboodle that most fetches my goat is the photo shoots that accompany the launch. We know football takes itself too seriously, but nothing confirms it more certainly than these surly, self-regarding line-ups.

You might imagine being a footballer is fun. You might even think being asked to pose for a few snaps with your mates might be a bit of a laugh. You would be wrong. The moment the latest breathable, fast-wicking, slightly-too-tight sweat-shop creation goes over their heads, every sensible player seems to think he has to channel Bruce Willis posing for the *Die Hard 5* poster, minus the irony.

Take the latest England kits from Nike, who seem determined to wring loyalty from supporters of the national team by the pound sterling. (If you've not seen them, a clue: one's white, the other's red.) In photos that took half a day out of one of Roy Hodgson's pre-World Cup get-togethers to shoot, Wayne Rooney, Joe Hart, Jack Wilshere, Daniel Sturridge and Steven Gerrard conspire to look like a gang you would cross the street to avoid rather than five of the nation's finest. Wilshere's even got his fist buried in the palm of his hand.

It is an undeniable fact of modern football that no player has ever smiled in a kit launch photo. Perhaps you have to gurn like a cheap movie extra or you get thrown out of the PFA. Or perhaps they have been told to look that way by marketing executives, who long ago decided that the only way football sells is with a snarl. The last thing they can afford is for a footballer to smile, least of all at themselves.

Paul is a Tottenham fan whose first game was at Highbury, which may explain a great deal of his subsequent capacity for endless pain and humiliation.

It is beyond reasonable doubt that a team's kit provides an umbilical cord with its supporters. The affinity fans have for their clubs' colours should never be messed with under any circumstances, yet we are faced with a constant stream of redesigns and subtle tweaks every season that render the replica kit bought at Christmas redundant; these are duly discarded in May, when the new edition is out. When kit becomes part of a brand-extension exercise, it is clear that the heart and soul are on the way out and are being replaced by profit and loss.

Oh when the Spurs go marching in – to Japan, China, Korea, Malaysia, etc. Probably one of the worst and most consistent crimes perpetuated by football clubs is this constant evolution that squeezes every last penny from their cash-strapped fans. Tottenham reached the depths of this shameful barrel when they announced, back in 2010, that there would be a different sponsor for Cup matches as opposed to the League. So the choice of shirts suddenly doubled, allowing THFC the chance to attract more commercial revenue while also fleecing the fans for another range of replica shirts, shorts and socks.

Chairman Daniel Levy justified the idea of 'secondary' sponsor AIA at the start of 2013/14 season by pointing out, 'We look forward to working closely with AIA over the coming season and introducing our club to more fans in AIA's home, the dynamic Asia-Pacific region.' Reading between the lines, Levy's statement might be interpreted as, 'We are delighted to open up lucrative new markets globally while at the same time stinging our customers at home.'

Levy and Spurs are not alone in using their kit as a means of slaking their thirst for the global dollar. Liverpool, for example, have signed a shirt deal with Warrior Sports, a US clothes brand that is worth a staggering £300 million over six years. The Boston-based company even had the temerity to suggest that the new kit is 'a modern take on the 1984 version, worn during the Club's fourth European Cup win'. So we have come full circle, as the latest kits echo the ones from three decades ago and the cash tills resound to the *ker-ching!* of the poor beleaguered fan as he desperately tries to keep up with the march towards global brand dominance.

L is for Loans

Neither a borrower, nor a lender be:
For loan oft loses both itself and friend.
From *Hamlet* by William Shakespeare

The idea of loaning players has been around for many years, and was originally a well-meaning move to allow players denied first team opportunities the chance to get some action under their belts. But the system has become corrupted somewhat as the big clubs flex their financial muscles. Like a show-off on the beach, they preen themselves in front of their puny adversaries. The likes of Chelsea and Manchester City have such vast resources and hugely inflated squads that they use the loan system as a means of offloading the excess baggage, while denying their rivals the opportunity of securing the long-term services of these players.

The prevailing attitude is that we have so much money that we can afford to maintain a massive squad, many members having no chance of playing for us. In April 2014, Chelsea had enough players out on loan to assemble an alternative twenty-five-man squad and more. It was therefore quite a twist of fate that Chelsea's shock home defeat to Sunderland, which effectively ended their title ambitions, was mainly down to two players on loan from close rivals Liverpool and Arsenal, with Borini scoring the winning goal and Mannone excelling in goal. The biter was well and truly bit.

For the most ludicrous example of the loan system, look no further than Thibaut Courtois, the Belgian goalkeeper. Chelsea bought him from Genk in July 2011 on a five-year deal and then within a matter of weeks he was shipped off to Atlético Madrid on loan, where he has been ever since. Courtois has played over a hundred games for Atlético, which is over a hundred more than he has played for Chelsea. His first game at Stamford Bridge was for Atlético, in the Champions League semi-final, when he ensured Atlético's progress at Chelsea's expense. Courtois has also represented his country over a dozen times, but he has never played a single minute for his parent club. This is plainly ludicrous, and, recognising the absurdity of the situation, Courtois has quite justifiably asked to get this charade sorted out once and for all. The club is being forced into offering a new contract to a player who has not stepped on to the pitch for them once in three years. Maybe a case of a new television show format in the offing – 'I'm an international goalkeeper, get me out of here'?

When Atlético were drawn to play Chelsea in the Champions League semi-final, the thorny issue of a player coming up against his parent club was thrust into the limelight. UEFA were forced to declare their hand prior to the draw, making a statement about 'competition integrity', which basically gave the Spanish club permission to play Courtois. They dismissed any idea of a 'private contract' between the clubs in which team selection could be influenced as 'null, void and unenforceable as far as UEFA are concerned'. That the governing body had to make such a statement suggests that something had been agreed in a smoke-filled room between London and Madrid, and such collusion was not allowed.

Another of Chelsea's multitude of loanees, the young full-back Ryan Bertrand – who, after all, is a full England international and has a Champions League winners' medal from 2012 – was also deemed surplus to requirements. Bertrand was consequently shipped off to Villa Park in January 2014 for his troubles, despite his impressive performance in that Champions League final. With over 150 senior appearances to his name, Bertrand is an experienced campaigner, but more than four-fifths of those games have been while he was on loan.

Alongside such high-profile youngsters, there is a batch of players with Dutch side Vitesse, which has effectively become a feeder club for Chelsea. This cosy relationship has been brought to the attention of the Dutch FA after the allegation from former chairman Merab Jordania that Chelsea actively discouraged Vitesse from qualifying for the Champions League, as it would compromise the UEFA rule that two teams under the same ownership cannot compete. Chelsea deny the accusation, but those smoke-filled rooms certainly seem to be seeing a fair bit of action.

We have now reached the point where Chelsea, or Manchester City for that matter, could assemble a team of loanees packed to the gunnels with internationals that would perform creditably in the Premier League. That team could certainly hold their own among the top-division teams and would probably finish in the top half of the table, and that is just not right in any way. With money and resources so polarised, the concept of a 'level playing field' has all but disappeared, and the oligopoly at the top is destined to remain, aided and abetted by the ludicrous, unfettered loan system. The alarming prospect of the larger clubs' reserve teams competing in the League moved ever closer when the FA announced it was being considered as part of Greg Dyke's commission. It is little wonder that loyalty has become such a scarce commodity; the players are increasingly treated as mere chattels by the owners and managers, to be moved hither and thither.

The loan system has something of 'the Wild West' about it, according to Martin Samuel of the *Daily Mail*. Samuel explains that with the loan system operating under its own jurisdiction, neatly sidestepping Financial Fair Play rules and favouring the big guns, this is football's equivalent of the O.K. Corral. Thus, Everton can attract the varied and valued talents of Lukaku, Deulofeu and Barry from Chelsea, Barcelona and Manchester City without having to shell out around £50 million in permanent fees, and nobody, apart from Wenger, bats an eyelid. The idea of assembling a squad based around loanees is not against the rules, but it does smack of short-term expediency. However, anything goes in the race for a Champions League spot, as Arsenal should know, having loaned out fourteen players during the 2013/14 season.

It is difficult to envisage any other business, or indeed sport, that encourages the wholesale transfer of assets on such a grand scale, and all on a temporary basis, to suit the short-term benefits of a few to the detriment of the many. Or, as Samuel succinctly put it, some clubs are 'running a shop with someone else's stock'. To illustrate the madness of this stockpiling of players, the position at Serie A club Parma takes some beating. As of April 2014, Parma had a quite incredible roster of players on loan to other clubs, numbering over 200 strewn across the lower reaches of Italy and other European leagues, plus over forty players who are 'co-owned'. It all makes a mockery of this fundamentally flawed system that owes much to the principle of feudal times when the wealthy dished out alms to the less fortunate, namely those who were lower down the pecking order. The crucial difference is that almsgivers were doing it out of the goodness of their hearts, whereas Chelsea *et al.* are effectively tidying up their books so that they do not fall foul of Financial Fair Play.

L is for Loyalty

> A prince should employ his minister according to the rules of propriety; ministers should serve their prince with faithfulness (loyalty).
>
> Confucius

The concept of loyalty within football is seemingly a relic of the past, having gone the same way as baggy shorts and rattles. It has become a sepia-tinted memory that belongs in a museum for future generations to marvel and look at from afar. As loyalty has become less and less a feature of the game, the notion of the 'one-club man' has correspondingly receded into oblivion. In a world dominated by Agents, Bosman and Cash, the twenty-first century's ABC actively encourages the movement of players between clubs. The stalwart who plays for one club and one club only is something of a rarity.

Ryan Giggs' longevity at Manchester United is considered to be almost freakish in nature, and even he started out as a youth player with rivals City before moving to Old Trafford. Giggs' retirement as a player at the end of the 2013/14 season brought to a close a career that lasted almost a quarter of a century. For many, over twenty-four months at any one club is now regarded as a long stretch, let alone twenty-four years. Furthermore, up to May 2014 only nineteen managers out of the ninety-two league clubs had been in situ for longer than two years. With the average lifespan of a Premier League manager now only marginally ahead of the mayfly, there are very few role models of club loyalty to follow.

Such is the prevalent attitude of instability that it seems as though there is something amiss if a player is not itching for a move within a year of joining a club, or if a manager is not looking nervously over his shoulder after a second successive defeat. Loyalty to the cause is undermined by the short-term nature of the relationships between clubs and their employees. Total allegiance to the cause is expected, but aren't these demands for loyalty unrealistic, idealistic and, quite frankly, slightly naïve? Why should fans expect players and managers to stick with their clubs when the majority are treated like cattle – very well-paid cattle, admittedly – to be traded in when they are past their best, or even before they have even had a chance to prove themselves?

In most other occupations, freedom of movement is part and parcel of the work contract, but footballers have had to battle for such rights. What if a player, or even a manager, decides to treble his salary by upping sticks and going to another club? The man is not a Judas, as some would readily claim; he is merely improving his lot, and going a long way to securing his financial future, as anyone would do in similar circumstances. Demanding total loyalty and being blind to opportunities elsewhere is tantamount to a restriction of trade, and is unworkable. The plain truth is that supporters are stuck with their clubs but players and managers are not, and they move on with increasing regularity. It is sad but true that we live in fickle times, when loyalty has become an outmoded principle and should be neither expected nor demanded.

M is for Music

If music be the food of love, play on;
Give me excess of it, that, surfeiting,
The appetite may sicken, and so die.
From *Twelfth Night* by William Shakespeare

If there were two aspects of life that should never be mixed then music and football are those elements. The history of pairing football and music is littered with so many discordant moments and so few successes that it is a small wonder that people still strive to achieve it. But try they do, and keep trying, and inevitably they will fail. In theory it is such a wonderful idea, matching the highs and lows of football with the peaks and troughs of music. Musicians and footballers have a natural affinity as high-profile performers, whose short-lived careers often crash and burn. George Best was known as the Fifth Beatle, and he was part of pop culture of the 1960s. There is a mutual love between the two worlds that suggests it should work. But, in practice, all these sorry, pitiful attempts end up in a horrific series of dog's dinners.

As one of the few high points of such collaboration was the appearance of Stuart Pearce's picture on the inside sleeve of The Lurkers' album *God's Lonely Men*, it suggests that this is not a marriage made in heaven. All due respect to Psycho for his alternative credibility, but Pearce would find himself very much on his own in the changing room, full of much more mainstream and mundane choices.

And that is pretty much that in terms of positive examples of music and football mixing well. The problem is where to start in plucking examples from the endless reservoir of disasters that lie strewn among the many tales of not-so-heroic failure. With so much material to work from, how does one start to select from such a cornucopia of crap? But if in doubt, let's begin at the very top and with the greatest tournament on earth, the World Cup, which has its own deeply troubled history.

My earliest vivid memories of the World Cup (see 'E is for England') go back to Mexico 1970 and the England song 'Back Home', which is still firmly lodged in my frontal cortex, like a scar that never heals. The lyrics were not exactly in the Lennon and McCartney bracket, although they did suggest that the nation was fully supportive of the team while they were so far away, which was heartwarming.

This was the first time the England football team had recorded a World Cup song, and the single – unlike the first Beatles single, which only got to No. 48 in the charts – reached the giddy heights of No. 1 in the UK. Fuelled no doubt by a strong sense of our invincibility, 'Back Home' stayed at the top of the pops for three weeks in May before that deflating quarter-final loss to West Germany, and just as we struggled to take it all in, the squad were indeed, as predicted, back home.

Thankfully for all music lovers, England failed to qualify for the next two World Cups, but 1982's fatalistic title 'This Time We'll Get It Right' reached new, unknown depths of inane lyrical vacuity with its opening lines. They underlined the fact that there were twenty-two members of Ron Greenwood's squad and they were more than ready to deliver the goods. The inevitable *Schadenfreude* followed this mighty call to arms, and England's Spanish jaunt petered out after a tame 0-0 with the hosts. Unbowed, 1986's effort invited further ridicule and laughter; 'We've Got the Whole World at Our Feet' would have been comic if it hadn't come up against the travesty of Maradona's Hand of God.

The paucity of talent that was so glaringly obvious in these ham-fisted attempts at musical and sporting harmony was brutally exposed by the next pair in line. Realisation had finally dawned on the powers-that-be that such sensitive things as pop songs should be left to professionals. So in 1990 we were treated to The Farm's anthem 'All Together Now', as well as New Order's 'World in Motion'. The former was typical indie fare, but it was hardly Premier League, hovering at the top of League One, at best lower Championship standard. On the other hand, the latter stands out as possibly the only World Cup song that bears repeating, although John Barnes' rap takes the shine off its rare quality.

Like 'Back Home', its predecessor of twenty years, 'World in Motion' made it to No. 1 and remains New Order's only chart-topper, which adds a dose of irony to the affair. It was also the band's last recording for Factory Records and certainly the last World Cup song worth pressing. We do not need to dwell on subsequent releases, but suffice it to say that 1998 saw the release of 'Vindaloo', which represented the end of the line in so many ways. Sensibly, the Football Association acknowledged the state of play by declaring that there would be no World Cup song for the 2010 campaign and the nation breathed a massive, collective sigh of relief.

Unfortunately, World Cup songs are not isolated examples of pop and football coming together and falling apart. The sorry saga continues with FA Cup songs. The earliest FA Cup ditties go back to the 1930s when, rather quaintly, each finalist appeared on either side of the single. The 1970s produced even worse aberrations than their World Cup cousins, as they appeared more frequently; the annual travail took parochialism to a new, unheard-of level. To name a few will give plentiful evidence of the shocking nature of these sorry, shameful shanties.

The 'Anfield Rap' of 1988 was so bad that even the surprising humiliation at the hands of Wimbledon at Wembley did not mask the true horror of a song that contained almost indescribable lyrics. They had the temerity to suggest that had Napoleon aped the Liverpool Way, we might even now be living under French rule.

Matching that for crassness somehow was Tottenham's 1981 paean to their Argentine midfielder Ardiles, who will probably never shake off the ignominy of Chas and Dave's refrain that he was off to Wembley and as a result his knees had turned all trembley (*sic*) or having to lisp that he was representing Totting-ham in true *'Allo 'Allo!* style. A year later, when the Falklands War started, the notion that Spurs were sending their soldiers to Wembley under General Burkinshaw may well have haunted him further. Irrespective of these cringeworthy disasters, the compulsion to produce an FA Cup song has not gone away, and further embarrassment is destined to be heaped upon clubs in their hours of triumph. Forget Chas and Dave, these are chalk and cheese.

But this hall of shame would not be complete without mention of a collaboration that promised so much but delivered so little. Both were extremely gifted players, enjoyed luxuriant hairstyles and even had rhyming surnames. After all this, they came together to produce possibly one of the most pitiful records of all time. Need I say more than 'diamond lights', Glenn and Chris?

Outside these recorded atrocities, there is the cacophonous issue of stadium music, because the PA systems have been turned up to eleven, in Spinal Tap speak. The ear-bleeding volume accentuates the often poorly chosen selection of the people responsible for the music. At times, it seems as if we have been transported into a time warp. The last few decades appear to have been swept away and forgotten as we are suddenly landed back in the 1980s, with such stone-cold classics as Rick Astley coming from nowhere with 'Never Gonna Give You Up' – and who could forget Survivor's 'Eye of the Tiger'? Certainly not the stadium DJ.

Apart from those at the clubs, perhaps the worst offenders are those at Wembley who trot out 'We are the Champions' or 'Simply the Best' without any sense of shame. The deafening noise reaches such a crescendo that it makes your teeth rattle, which gives them some relief from being permanently gritted. The poor sods whose team have won the respective trophy have to sit through fifteen minutes of this tripe; at least the losers have the consolation of trekking off down Wembley Way without having their senses assailed by such bilge, a sop to their disappointment.

Even some of the giants of football are sucked into this vortex of bad music, as can be illustrated by Pep Guardiola, who has been at the helm of two of Europe's greatest club sides and who has produced some of the most mesmerising and successful football of the last decade. On his arrival at the German champions in 2013, he let slip that one of his first actions would be an attempt to influence their music choice. 'Of course I will introduce the players to Coldplay – I just hope they have good musical taste.' Such a statement just goes to prove that nobody is perfect, and even those at the pinnacle have chinks in their armour.

An additional element of the music–football mix that

grates beyond all others has to be the Champions League theme tune. Grandiose, pretentious and infuriating are some of the gentler comments expressed over this reworking of Handel's Coronation anthem, originally entitled 'Zadok the Priest'. I am not sure who Zadok was, but I am pretty sure he would not want to have anything to do with the 'jazzing up' in Tony Britten's arrangement of 1992, and Handel will no doubt be turning in his grave and covering his ears. Consider the opening lyrics, which are almost impossible to make out and for a good reason. The catchy ditty explains that these are not just the best teams, but the very best; it's a handy reminder that the upcoming ninety minutes represent the main event. That BBC 5 Live commentator Alan Green finds this inspiring sums it all up.

The last bum note in this lamentable medley of music and football is left to a song that has been besmirched by its association with football. The Verve's 'Bitter Sweet Symphony' is one of the better indie anthems, and, despite the accusations of plagiarism over its sampling of The Rolling Stones' 'The Last Time', it was one of those tunes that neatly summed up that period. But that was before someone at ITV Sport had the bright idea of using this as the backing track to their coverage of England internationals. The association with the world of Adrian Chiles, Andy Townsend *et al.* has completely changed the song, to such an extent that hearing the opening chords with its searing violins no longer takes us back to golden memories of the late 1990s but brings on the cold sweats and shaking of watching the national team (see 'E is for

England'). I am sure that Richard Ashcroft is delighted to see the royalties rolling in every time England are on ITV, but even he must baulk and shiver a little bit as his best-loved song lives up to its title. An extremely bittersweet symphony, indeed.

M is for Mascots

> A mascot needs to stand for something. It needs to be more than just cute – it has to have a personality.
>
> Don Carter, American sportsman/commentator

As ostensibly regular representatives of their clubs, even ambassadors, mascots do not cover themselves in glory. They are quite often a major source of embarrassment and ridicule. The very idea of dressing up in a life-sized suit and frightening small children would usually get you a quick pass to the local penitentiary or lunatic asylum. Here is a typical reaction to one of these mascots from Arsenal fan Nick Laney, who describes the terror his two sons endured at the hands of Gunnersaurus:

> Nobody, not even those they are allegedly there to please, understands football mascots. Took both my boys to their first games when they were four years old (surely the prime demographic?) and they were both openly disdainful of Gunnersaurus. My youngest, quite sensibly, enquired why Barney the Dinosaur's bastard child was at the game.

5. You cannot possibly miss Gunnersaurus, Arsenal's official mascot, however much you may want to. Of all the dinosaurs, why was he the only one to survive?

Even the players have been known to shun Gunnersaurus, as witnessed before the 2014 FA Cup semi-final when Bacary Sagna dodged his handshake with a look of incredulous disdain that summed up all Arsenal fans' feelings. Maybe the real reason behind the French full-back's departure had as much to do with his opinion of Gunnersaurus as with Arsene Wenger. That Gunnersaurus wears Nike-emblazoned boots and has his very own blog to further poison young people's minds is possibly a matter that needs to be raised in Parliament.

My own son has often queried the sanity of a grown man masquerading as Pete the Eagle when we have the real-life Kayla to swoop up and down the pitch at Selhurst Park in the pre-match ritual. For many years the man behind the costume was the headmaster of a school in Kent, and I am not sure if the school governors approved of his avian escapades at the weekends, but it surely should have been raised as a point of some urgency. Also, the fact that Pete has a partner, Alice, is equally disturbing to adults and children alike. With so much indignity flying around, it seems unpardonable to encourage such behaviour, but there is even an annual Mascots Grand National race, which goes beyond the bounds of human decency in forcing these unnatural, disturbing creatures even further into our consciousness. This is the stuff of nightmares, and they must be resisted, or else civilisation will be over as we know it. Beware the march of the mascots.

One of the few occasions when the mascots have shown their true colours was when there was a spat between Wolfie, representing Wolves, and a couple of Bristol City mascots at Ashton Gate in late 1998. The little contretemps began as some playful joshing, but ended up in a full-on bust-up with punches being thrown, and ended in a dressing down for the over-aggressive Wolfie while the City Cat was thrown out of the ground.

This eye witness statement from Dave Singleton, a Bristol City fan sums it all up:

> We all thought it was play-acting and the Wolves fans were cheering, but then it all went wrong when one of the pigs whacked Wolfie. There was another scuffle in

> the tunnel, and I saw Wolfie catch a pig with a left hook and the City Cat steamed in. Then the stewards marched them out.

Such behaviour finally exposed the tooth and claw nature of these supposedly family-friendly entertainers, and showed them for the animals we all know they are.

N is for Naming Rights

> The reputation which the world bestows is like the wind, that shifts now here now there, its name changed with the quarter whence it blows.
>
> From *The Divine Comedy* by Dante

The custom of selling naming rights to the highest bidder is one of those money-grabbing aspects of football; it tramples all over the proud heritage that clubs have established over a long time in the dash for a fast buck. The very idea of uprooting the traditional name of a ground and obliterating it for the sake of some commercial gain is abhorrent. Just ask Newcastle fans how they felt when Mike Ashley, in all his wisdom, decided that after over a hundred years it was time to rename St James' Park the Sports Direct Arena in November 2011. Even to non-Geordies it all seemed so wrong. The club's justification was that St James' Park was not 'commercially attractive'. One of the iconic names of English football was swept away, to 'showcase' the sponsorship potential that has been dormant for more than a century.

If this cavalier attitude to one of the oldest and best-loved stadiums is allowed to continue unchecked by decency then the future looks very bleak indeed. There are over a dozen sponsored stadia currently, and it is conceivable that in five years' time nearly every ground will have undergone a renaming and brands will have replaced those names rich in history. Imagine Liverpool no longer playing at Anfield but at Poundland Park, or Manchester United foregoing Old Trafford for the sake of the Marks & Spencer Stadium. It is a terrifying prospect, but it might just happen, so everyone with the true values of football in their hearts needs to be wary of this creeping up on them and biting them on the backside.

The hideous revolution was reversed a year later, when the little-loved and barely used Sports Direct Arena was abandoned and, on the insistence of a new sponsor, St James' Park was restored to its rightful place. But the very fact that it was allowed to happen in the first place is cause for concern, and there is no guarantee that there will not be another u-turn for the commercial benefit of the club. Added to which, the company that stepped in as sponsor and wound back the clock was none other than Wonga, a company that specialises in short-term fixes that invariably lead to long-term problems. How apt.

The venerable Jeff Stelling, everyone's favourite Saturday-afternoon host, voiced his own dismay at this mercenary attitude. The Sky Sports *Soccer Saturday* host has consistently refused to switch to calling the grounds by their new nomenclature. He is a stickler for tradition. 'Now, it's long been a bugbear of mine,' wrote Stelling, 'that sponsors are allowed to replace the historic name of a ground with their own name however transient their sponsorship is and there are plenty of examples over the years.'

So it is still Field Mill and Adams Park, not the One Call and Causeway stadiums. As Stelling points out, there are plenty of examples of clubs following the Faustian route of selling the soul of the club to the highest bidder. York City's Kit Kat Crescent remains the most bittersweet of renamings. Bootham Crescent used to conjure up muddy memories of noble FA Cup battles, toppling Arsenal, Keith Houchen and the like, but between 2005 and 2010 it was reduced to a piece of confectionery. The justification for this was that York was home to Nestlé, and that the red and white colours of both the club and the chocolate bar were in some way serendipitous and proved to be the most natural of fits.

Unfortunately this came in the wake of some excessive tinkering by previous owner and asset stripper extraordinaire, John Batchelor, whose keenness on a whole new image led to the shirt becoming a chequered monstrosity to fit in with his other main interest of touring cars. Batchelor even rejigged the club's name, reinventing them as York City Soccer Club. The embarrassment did not stop there, as Batchelor relayed recordings of Barcelona's crowd over the tannoy in an attempt to recreate the atmosphere of Camp Nou – or maybe that should have been Camp Nougat. Not content with such radical revisions, Batchelor also changed his own name to B&Q to attract sponsorship for his racing team.

At half time there would have been plentiful opportunities for the stadium announcer to encourage the crowd to have a break, have a Kit Kat break, but surely that was the only tangible benefit on offer apart from the filthy lucre. The fact that throughout this five-year deal with Nestle the Minstermen struggled and failed to return to the Football League pointed to a flaw in the grand plan. Within a couple of years of ridding themselves of the dreaded Kit Kat tag, dropping 'Soccer Club' and restoring Bootham to its rightful place, York City FC were on the rise and won the Conference Play-Offs in 2012 after a seven year exile. Surely a salutary lesson learned for all those who are tempted to toy with stadium re-branding. It does not work and never will be acceptable.

But despite everything still they keep doing it, as witnessed when Bolton Wanderers switched from one sports manufacturer to another and the Reebok Stadium suddenly became the Macron in July 2014. And so Burnden Park, their home for a hundred years, gets buried further under the weight of commercialism. There will now be Wanderers fans who no longer know or even care about their original stadium. Very soon there will be as many changes of stadium name as there are changes in kit, an ever revolving door of sponsors. With around a third of all English League grounds now carrying the name of commercial backers it will not be long before there are more renamed stadia than there are traditional names, which is a sad indication of how affairs have moved on since 1997, when the Reebok opened and became one of the first sponsored grounds in the country.

N is for Numbers (Squad)

I am not a number. I am a free man.
I am not a number. I am a person.
From *The Prisoner* television series

One of the more irritating innovations of recent years is the explosion of shirt numbers that has rendered the age-old system of 1 to 11 meaningless. The celebrated Huddersfield and Arsenal supremo Herbert Chapman was the pioneer who introduced the idea of shirt numbering in 1920s, and the league soon followed suit; for seventy-odd years, all was hunky-dory. But, in the 1993/94 season, the rules changed, allowing players the choice of numbers all the way up to 99; such free choice led to the anarchy we are faced with today.

It would have been sacrilegious to suggest it previously, but a marauding defender or a deep-lying midfielder could now wear the iconic No. 10 shirt made famous by Pelé. We, the punters, have very little chance of making sense of the madness of this deregulated market. So rather than having your new centre forward displayed as a classic No. 9, the unveiling of the latest transfer comes with him holding aloft his No. 38 shirt in front of the expectant cameras. The fans are left scratching their heads, trying to work out whether as a No. 38 he plays in the diamond, or maybe in the hole behind the striker. The hope is that he might have a slight inkling of where the bloody hell he might end up on the pitch, but there is no guarantee.

Such latitude even extends to goalkeepers, who are granted *carte blanche* to mess with the natural order and who are allowed to shun the classic No. 1.

There is no more disorienting sight than seeing your first-choice goalie wearing a 77 on his back. Even one of the most astute of modern tacticians, Michael Cox, the editor and creator of Zonal Marking and freelance journalist, is befuddled by it all. Cox yearns for the age when you could rely on the simplicity of a standard set of numbers. For a man who can spot a false number nine from a hundred paces or detect a shift from 4-4-2 to 4-5-1 in the blink of an eye, this throws an interesting and worrying light on where the ordinary fan stands now. Perplexed and confused would be at the more optimistic end of the spectrum.

Your number's up – Michael Cox

It is now two decades since the Football Association decided to abandon the use of 1–11 shirts, switching to a system of permanent squad numbers instead. Today, team sheets resemble bingo cards.

The importance of the traditional numbers has been lost. Manchester United, for example, had no number nine after Dimitar Berbatov's departure, but neither Javier Hernandez, nor Danny Welbeck nor Robin van Persie elected to take the shirt, instead sticking with 14, 19 and 20 respectively. Perhaps they were scared by the example of Antonio Valencia, who switched from 25 to 7 – the fabled number worn by David Beckham, Cristiano Ronaldo and George Best – but, after a poor campaign, returned to his more familiar 25.

A squad number is now part of a player's personal brand. Beckham later colonised 23, partly in tribute to Michael Jordan, and wore 32 when this wasn't available. Nicolas Anelka has worn 39 for Manchester City, Fenerbahce, Bolton, Chelsea, West Brom and even the French national side – which is particularly ludicrous considering France will never have a 39-man squad.

1–11 numbers, on the other hand, had historic significance. The unusual pattern of traditional shirt numbers in an English 4-4-2 formation relates back to the old 'Pyramid' system, or 2-3-5. From right to left, 2 and 3 were the defenders, 4, 5 and 6 midfielders and 7, 8, 9, 10 and 11 attackers. With the numbers 5, 6 and 8 dropping back once formations became more defensive, this explains why '7' continued to be the right-winger, and '9' the central striker, for example.

Shirt numbers were about a role, rather than an individual. AC Milan have boasted some fantastic 9–10 combinations through the years – Jose Altafini and Gianni Rivera, Ruud Gullit and Marco van Basten, George Weah

> and Zvonimir Boban, Pippo Inzaghi and Rui Costa. Now the tradition has been lost; Mario Balotelli wears 45 because 'it brings me luck', and Stephan El Shaarawy wears 92 to represent his year of birth.
>
> It sums up modern football's emphasis upon pandering to the needs of increasingly demanding superstars. This is a team sport, and players should be assigned numbers that reflect their role, not their personality.

Michael Cox's first match was at Highbury on Saturday 4 November 1995, Arsenal 1 Manchester United 0.

As Michael Cox rightly points out, aside from the confusion sown by the apparently random selection of numbers there is also the plucking of special numbers, such as David Beckham's preference for No. 23. When Beckham joined Real Madrid in 2003 he realised that the No. 7 was not available as it was the property of Real legend Raúl. The significance of 23 was not immediately apparent to us Brits; maybe it was a testimony to his epic England performance at Old Trafford against Greece when he was everywhere, inside forward, goalscorer and defensive midfielder all rolled into one. Thus the formula is 10 + 9 + 4 = 23. But the truth was that his wife Victoria had pointed out that this was the retired number of the one and only Michael Jordan. Behind every great man there is, of course, the likes of Victoria. So 23 was considered to be of sufficient gravitas for David to adopt for his own nascent galactic career. Quite how we are meant to translate Jordan's role on a basketball court into the intricacies of a 4-4-2 has never been fully explained, and probably will never be so. Considering the uproar that was created by Gianliugi Buffon's pick of 88, which led to accusations of a fascist subplot, it is probably better to let it lie.

O is for Ownership

So the industrious bees do hourly strive
To bring their loads of honey to the hive;
Their sordid owners always reap the gains,
And poorly recompense their toils and pains.
From *The Woman's Labour* by Mary Collier

The ideal football club owner would be rich, anonymous and kind-hearted. Just imagine a wealthy philanthropist who was publicity shy, with the good of the club forever etched in his soul. Alas, not many owners possess such a mixture of attributes, and in fact two out of those three is a rarity; a fair number fail entirely to getting close to possessing even one. They are not quite as wealthy as was first imagined, forever preening themselves in the media and generally using the club as another rung in the ladder to their own personal success. Talk to any fan, and they will invariably have a tale of woe about one of their owners being a rogue, a bankrupt or a criminal, and quite possibly all three rolled into one.

Many point to the influx of foreign owners as the ruin of the game, but that is bordering on xenophobic and desperately wide of the mark. The notion of the generous benefactor who bestows his wealth on his hometown team is all rather quaint and slightly delusional. For every Jack Walker, who lavished his personal wealth on turning Blackburn into Premier League champions, there are dozens of undesirables, who arrive awash with promises but suck the lifeblood of the club and leave it in a perilous state, penniless and pointless.

It is the crushing inevitability of what happens that is so deplorable. The fans can smell a rat as soon as the new owners arrive, but are powerless to do anything about it. The first warning sign that alerts everyone to the forthcoming demise of their club is when the new chairman declares that he is taking them all the way to the top. The Premier League beckons for the mid-table League Two outfit within the space of five years, according to the incoming messiah. Exuding unfounded confidence, it is a matter of when, not if, the glory days will return.

The hollow words that 'we won't be in this division for long' often bounce back to hurt everyone, with the team hurtling out of the Football League and towards the Conference with alarming speed. Then, of course, there is the declaration of a vision (see 'V is for Vision'), which clouds the issue for a while; fans scratch their heads and wonder how on earth this could ever become a reality, given the poor-playing squad allied with the decay and decline endured over the previous ten years. The final nail in the coffin is hammered home when the new man in charge starts going misty-eyed over his first match on the terraces in the 1960s, and it is at this juncture that it is time to don the sackcloth and ashes, while making alternative plans for Saturday afternoons.

Take the sorry tale of Blackburn. After the unprecedented success of the Walker reign, the current Venky's regime bought the club in 2010 from the Walker family trust and has reduced the club to a shadow of its former self. There was much confusion and bemusement among Blackburn fans when Venky's arrived, as they had no record of being involved or even interested in football up to the point of their purchase and have shown little of either ever since. Results have been disappointing to say the least, and they now face their third season in the Championship, with little prospect of a return to the Premier League.

But it is the dislocation between the owners and the club's board and fans that sets them apart and reduced the club to a laughing stock, with adviser Shebby Singh as chief clown. The only table they have managed to top over the last few years has been the survey of worst-run clubs, which was hotly contested. The Indian-based poultry firm has taken internal squabbling (or maybe that should be clucking) to a new level, with managers on a furiously spinning merry-go-round and the board not quite sure where they stand. This was exposed by a letter from Paul Hunt, the deputy chief executive. In light of their impending relegation from the top division in the 2011/12 season, Hunt outlined the internecine wars that were ripping the club apart and how Rovers were suffering terribly, and that he and his co-directors could lose their homes as a result of the mess engulfing the club.

But this type of farcical ownership is not something that we solely import, as there are plenty of ruinous British owners, both past and present, who have taken over clubs and then brought them to their knees with their shameful mismanagement amid a variety of nefarious activities. It is a veritable rogues' gallery of the not-so-good, the really bad and the extremely ugly. Of the several basket cases, perhaps George Reynolds, formerly of the parish of Darlington, is the man with the most form to his name. Before Reynolds took over at Darlington he had already been imprisoned a few times in his youth, and he showed little inclination to reform when he became owner in 1999. After building a 25,000-capacity stadium to house an average crowd of 4,000, the club unsurprisingly went into administration, and eventually went out of the Football League and then out of business. Meanwhile, Reynolds was arrested with £500,000 in cash tucked into the boot of his car, convicted of tax evasion and was back in jail for another stretch behind bars, much to the relief of all right-minded Darlington fans.

David Preece was a young goalkeeper with Darlington in the Reynolds era, and he suffered first hand from the machinations of his chairman, as he elucidates in a piece he wrote for *Sabotage Times*.

I was there on the exact day that Darlington Football Club began its cruelly slow and painful slide into the black hole of extinction. Over the last thirteen years, the Darlo fans must have felt as if their beloved club had been gradually destroyed, like a live pig being excruciatingly spit roasted to a mere block of black charcoal.

The arrival of convicted safecracker turned multi-millionaire businessman George Reynolds was supposed to be the dawn of a bright new era. I was the twenty-one-year-old goalkeeper for the Quakers and like everyone else I was initially caught up in the whirlwind of promises to build a brand-spanking-new stadium and bring us Premier League football within five years. I say 'initially' because for me, the cracks presented themselves rather early in his reign. Of course, I couldn't foresee the agonising years the club has since endured but I could sense something didn't add up.

Unsurprisingly, Reynolds is not the only chairman to have ended up in prison, and another member of legs eleven, Owen Oyston, infamously sacked Sam Allardyce as Blackpool manager while in jail awaiting trial. Oyston ended up with a six-year sentence for rape and indecent assault in 1996. His son, Karl, took over the reins at Bloomfield Road, and his continuing unpopularity with the fans reached a head after he claimed that money was not important in football to justify why there had been such limited expenditure on players since they had tasted Premier League action in 2010/11. This was despite the fact that his father had been paid £11 million during that solitary Premier League season, more than the manager and his entire squad combined. When your dad is the recipient of such a large dollop of cash, is it any wonder that you get the feeling that money is so unimportant?

As it is clear from some of these *enfants terribles*, football ownership has attracted more than its fair share of demons, but the very worst are those owners who insist on meddling in the running of the football side. Not content to have made a complete horlicks of the business side, the truly megalomaniacal among them decide that they can do a better job than the manager. It starts with the odd appearance in the dressing room to pick over the bones of the latest demoralising defeat. But soon this minor faux pas progresses to a showdown with the manager, who is told that the time has come to shuffle him out of the door and let the chairman show how it should be done.

The late Ron Noades once told me in an interview that he was the best scout that Palace had ever had, and to prove his credentials he once took over as Brentford boss in 1998, and, in gaining promotion that season, he set the very dangerous precedent of a successful owner-manager model. Owners need absolutely no encouragement to start meddling into team affairs, but fortunately not too many have followed in Noades' footsteps as yet and made the transition from boardroom to boot room, although you can be sure that there are plenty who are itching to do so. Let the owners own and the managers manage, and then everyone will be moderately unhappy with their lot, free to resort to moaning about the crap manager and the shady owner, as tradition dictates.

P is for Plastics

> His strongest tastes were negative. He abhorred plastics, Picasso, sunbathing and jazz – everything in fact that had happened in his lifetime.
>
> From *The Ordeal of Gilbert Pinfold* by Evelyn Waugh

I am pretty sure Evelyn Waugh did not have the idea of plastic fans in mind when describing Gilbert Pinfold's tastes, but he should have, because this breed of humanity is among the lowest forms of humanity. Plastics have been called many derogatory names in the past, with glory hunters or armchair fans being a couple of the more gentle sobriquets. Plastics ostensibly support a club, but actually they follow from afar, very rarely go to matches and will turn their allegiance on and off depending upon results or other more pressing concerns. Their attitude to defeat is to shrug and move on, whereas, for genuine fans, they take any loss as a personal insult because it goes straight to the heart.

And there is the rub; it is all about the heart or the heartless. Without the emotional bond, there is nothing to supporting a club. Plastics are fickle, feckless human beings who feel nothing and treat football as a fad, which will eventually be replaced by something more shiny and attractive. Plastics move on, whereas real supporters have no choice; stuck with their plight, they soldier on manfully as their loyalty is sorely tested but never wavers.

Steve Browett, co-chairman and co-owner of Crystal Palace, highlights the difference between the two types of fan in relation to Manchester United and the so-called 'We Brigade'.

His first match was at Selhurst Park in the 1969/70 season, and although he cannot remember exactly, he thinks the opposition were Leeds United, which coincidentally was my first Palace match; my abiding memory from the game was the snarling ginger ball of fury that was Billy Bremner, who could never be accused of being plastic.

The 'We Brigade' – Steve Browett

I frequently get introduced to friends of friends and football inevitably seems to come up in conversation. When told that I've got something to do with Palace, they volunteer that they are 'a football fan' too. Nine times of ten, it's Manchester United, and I get all the stuff about 'we' won this and 'we' won that, and how great 'Giggsy', 'Scholesy' and 'Becks' were. Then they talk about 'Sir Alex' like he was their Dad, and how terrible Moyes is, because they've actually lost a few games this season. One such individual told me recently that he might start supporting

City if United don't qualify for the Champions League. Needless to say, these people are from places like Croydon or Bournemouth and have never been to Manchester, let alone Old Trafford. Instead of supporting their local team and actually going to games, they just drone on about how great it was when 'we' were Champions every year, and how terrible it must be to support a 'little' team like Palace that doesn't win very often. I really do hate them. I'm not joking.

It would not be fair to simply single out Manchester United; there are plastics at every club, although United do have more than their fair share. According to some market research, conducted by Kantar in 2011, United have a total of 659 million adult fans worldwide. A conservative estimate calculates that, if every one of those fans wanted to see United play just once at Old Trafford, they would need to play 8,693 matches, or 229 full Premier League seasons.

To rub salt into gaping wounds, Google Plus recently offered the chance for United fans to appear on advertising hoardings at the games, giving rise to a new type of fan – the digital plastic. The main advantage for the club is that this fan does not need any stewarding, and maybe opens up the utopian vision of a purely digital crowd. This is an audience that can be tracked and monitored, and of course sold to, without the hassle of going to the stadium, and is ripe for any sponsors' marketing message flashed on screen. One can just imagine the maniacal cackle of the finance guys at Old Trafford when they realised just what they had stumbled on.

On the rare occasion that these loathsome beings manage to attend a match they will spend most of the time on their phones or laptops, no doubt tweeting their 'experiences' or checking the scores for the other three clubs that they follow so avidly. Then, irrespective of the state of the match, which may be reaching a nerve-tingling climax with the result hanging in the balance, they are off and away 'to miss the crush' and be first out of the car park. There is no hint of shame as they scurry away, leaving behind rows of empty seats and hollow promises in the dash for the exit.

Plastics also bring with them a fair amount of baggage, and are prone to one of the most heinous crimes that can be committed within the environs of a football ground. Indeed, so bad is this behaviour that there is a very lively and active twitter account dedicated to unearthing these miscreants. Welcome to the world of Half Scarf Twats. This group seem to have no problem whatsoever with wearing a scarf that is split between the two competing clubs, and it beggars belief that such a practice is so widespread. Originally, the trend was started for Cup finals to mark the occasion of these momentous matches, which was bad enough, but now there are half scarves available for even the most pedestrian and prosaic matches. As plastics are prone to MSA – Multiple Support Affliction – it is fitting that they should indulge in some brazen Half Scarfing.

Another distressing addition to the plastics' armour is the preponderance of puerile paraphernalia. Unnecessary items that should be banned include giant foam hands, clappers, and the lowest of the low, those infuriating jester's hats. After extensive research, I still could not find anyone culpable for introducing the concept of foam hands to football, and it is no surprise that nobody will admit to being involved. Whatever possessed that anonymous, dark-hearted person that it was a good idea to produce these abominations in the first place should be isolated and put in a very deep hole. One has to assume that it was intended to be mildly amusing, but there is absolutely no redeeming feature about these ghastly appendages and any sentient being feels immediately nauseous at the mere sight of one. If the original perpetrator is ever tracked down then being hanged, drawn and quartered is barely adequate as a punishment. Chopping their hands off would be more fitting, if not quite severe enough.

Next in line for castigation are clappers, and I will leave it to Gus Poyet to expand on why these irritants should never ever be allowed near a football match. They almost define plasticity, in that they are meant to create an atmosphere in a fake fashion. They are so wrong in every way, and here is Poyet's righteous and justified response to their use at the play-offs semi-final in May 2013, in an internal email to Brighton & Hove Albion's staff in the wake of their 2-0 loss to Palace.

> It was an extremely silly idea and the result was an annoying noise. I am not for one minute blaming the

result of the game on this, but it added only negative vibes to the proceedings.

Just so, Gus; as if losing to your most bitter rivals at home in a crucial match was not enough, the unpleasant taste of defeat was exacerbated by those dreaded, puerile clappers. Maybe there should be a campaign to introduce a points deduction for any club who distribute clappers to their fans, as surely it is much more disgraceful than going into administration and more deserving of punitive action.

How much more humiliating was it for Chris Hughton that his departure from Norwich, with five matches remaining of the 2013/14 season, was accompanied by a barrage of yellow clappers thrown from the Carrow Road crowd? Clack off, they seemed to be saying, after the West Brom defeat in early April. Sure enough, by the end of the weekend, Hughton was gone, with the sight of clappers raining down on him as the lasting image of his two-year managerial reign. Hughton seems to be a thoroughly decent man who deserved so much more than this sorry, pitiful epitaph.

Right down in the basement along with the ghastly clappers are those frightful plastic flags that mercifully only turn up at big events such as Cup finals. Possibly the tackiest of all the tat that is assembled in the name of support, they are so flimsy and feeble that it is a surprise if they last through the match. They will sometimes be used when the Mexican wave is started (see 'W is for Wave'), but their fate is to be strewn, discarded and unloved, under the seats or in the surrounding streets after the crowds have long departed, just so much flotsam and jetsam.

One of the sure signs of being a plastic is the most deplorable habit ever witnessed within a public place. The frightening sight of inane waving and excessive smiling if the camera ever happens to spot them is enough to make the stomach churn. It is the sort of behaviour that may just be acceptable at a One Direction concert, but never in a football ground. The 'look at me, I am on the big screen' attitude is not only horrendously egocentric, but also characteristic of someone who has little or no interest in what is happening on the pitch. In an ideal world, the stewards would immediately eject anyone portraying such plasticity, and the club would then impose a life ban to keep them off our screens and out of our lives. They can also take their giant foam hands, face paints, plastic flags and clappers with them to the hottest inferno imaginable, where they will melt in a trice. Then they will no longer infect football with their poisonous artificiality and asinine customs.

Q is for Qatar 2022

Few men have virtue to withstand the highest bidder.
Letter by George Washington, 17 August 1779

Football authorities around the world will never win any popularity contests. They are generally vilified and mocked by fans, who rail against long periods of indecisiveness, but as soon as the authorities do make a decision they are roundly castigated for it. FIFA sits at the very apex, and cops for a fair amount of flak as it oversees the game from its Zurich headquarters.

At the very top sits the president, Sepp Blatter, who has ruled over his fiefdom (or should that be FIFA-dom?) for the last eighteen years with a mixture of arrogance and antipathy, reminiscent of a particularly wicked baron from the Middle Ages. Very few people in the know have a kind word to say about those running the show, or the organisation itself. Those that have the temerity to criticise the most powerful sports authority on the globe will have the modern equivalent of burning oil poured over them from a dizzy height.

FIFA's Hall of Shame is a long and dark one, with the corridors of power spreading like tentacles from their midst and enveloping all around them. There is a trail of disastrous and despicable decisions, which range from a lack of action taken against persistent racist offenders to the idea that female footballers should be made to wear skimpier clothing. As a reminder of quite how asinine Blatter can be, here is his master plan for how to spice up women's football from 2004.

'Let the women play in more feminine clothes like they do in volleyball,' he proposed. 'They could, for example, have tighter shorts. Female players are pretty, if you excuse me for saying so, and they already have some different rules to men – such as playing with a lighter ball. That decision was taken to create a more female aesthetic, so why not do it in fashion?' The idea that this is somehow justified by the rules of fashion exposes Blatter's dubious motives. These are sportspeople, not catwalk models.

But among the catalogue of frightful errors of judgement, various lapses of taste and generally indecent behaviour there is one decision that stands out as particularly reprehensible. The awarding of the World Cup in 2022 to Qatar must rank as the crassest action of a much maligned organisation. In fact, so bad was it that even Blatter reluctantly admitted that it may have been a mistake; he even turned slightly philosophical in his assessment. 'Of course, it's an error,' he said in an interview with Swiss television. 'You know, everyone makes mistakes in life.' So if Blatter can see it, as well as owning up to it, then it must be one hell of a blunder. When questioned whether the World Cup could be taken away from Qatar, he responded that he 'was not a prophet', which is tantamount to admitting that it is under serious consideration. And so it should be.

When Qatar was awarded the World Cup in December 2010 there was a genuine sense of shock throughout the football world, and the reverberations are still echoing four years on. Blatter's immediate defence was to roll out the well-worn argument that this was all part of a grand design to involve smaller countries. Giving the less developed nations the chance to spread the gospel is part of Blatter's mantra. The inherent problem with this ever-so-noble stance is that Qatar is not exactly a hotbed of football. It has neither a domestic league of any note nor a national team with any history of qualification from previous tournaments. Qatar was second-bottom of the Asian qualifying group for 2014, with their only victories coming against the might of Lebanon. The fact that Qatar won the bidding process by a country mile, against such strong, credible candidates as the United States, Australia and Japan, not only raised the odd eyebrow but stirred up a storm of dissension.

The bitter taste of corruption has been on everyone's lips, as a series of allegations have since been launched over the bidding process and particularly the conduct of certain members of the Executive Committee. In May 2011, the former chairman of England's bid to host the 2018 World Cup, Lord Triesman, tabled specific allegations in Parliament about the conduct of six members of FIFA's

Executive Committee during the bid process. Subsequent investigations into these and a string of other allegations have been hampered by the fact that nearly half of the Executive Committee's twenty-two members have since left their roles, several under a cloud of suspicion.

As serious questions continue to be raised, the scrutiny of the process intensifies, with all those members involved in the bid due to be grilled by the head of FIFA's ethics commission, Michael Garcia, the former FBI investigator. The cast list of shadowy figures in this web of intrigue includes the likes of Jack Warner and Mohamed bin Hammam, who have both made ignominious exits from FIFA. Disgraced erstwhile vice-president Warner resigned while suspended because allegations of bribery were being investigated. Meanwhile, Mohamed bin Hammam was banned from football for life in December 2012 after a separate vote-rigging scandal. And so it goes on, as FIFA resembles more a contemporary school for scandal than a reputable sport's governing body.

Since the award in 2010, the demand for some sort of reassessment, or even a rerun of the vote, has built into a concerted campaign to wrestle the World Cup from Qatar. The Executive Committee seemingly overlooked the insanity of playing a football tournament in temperatures of 50 degrees, having been reassured by the Qataris' promise of advanced cooling technologies. FIFA are now weighing up the option of moving the competition to the winter, for the very first time in the history of the World Cup. This is such a radical step that it defies belief that it had not been addressed as an issue.

Despite the fact that shifting the schedule would cause major disruption for all major European leagues as well as causing problems for the Africa Cup of Nations, which is scheduled to take place in January 2023, this is apparently a price worth paying, but not one that was taken into consideration during the bidding process. An element of due diligence would have surely raised serious questions.

Corporate governance is clearly not FIFA's strongest suit but surely it should be one of the defining attributes of a ruling body that makes such far-reaching and financially significant decisions. After all, they are responsible for the largest sporting event on the planet, not some shonky car boot sale or shabby school fête. Despite the road to Qatar being littered with corruption emanating from some of his charges, Blatter's self-belief appears impregnable, sailing along the surface of the murkiest waters with seemingly not a care in the world.

Blatter will point to how Qatar 2022 has broken the mould with a series of unique attributes. It is, by some margin, the smallest country to be awarded the World Cup, with a population of just over 2 million. It is the first country to host the World Cup that has never qualified for the tournament (apart from the original tournament in Uruguay in 1936). At its current ranking of 101, it is the first host country to be ranked outside the top 100 teams internationally. The year 2022 will be the first time the World Cup has been held in the Arab world, and also the first time that homosexuality is deemed illegal within the host country.

Blatter's response to the issue of sexuality was, as ever, as blunt as it was boorish, when he suggested that gay football fans should 'refrain from sexual activities'. This was apparently meant to be a joke, but it backfired and he was forced to apologise for causing offence. What is certainly not a joke is the treatment of workers involved in the construction of the stadiums, transport and general infrastructure projects. *The Guardian* uncovered in its 2013 investigation that there has already been a horrific toll on lives, with forty-four Nepalese workers dying in between 4 June and 8 August 2013 alone. 'The International Trade Union Conference has warned that at least 4,000 migrant workers could die in the construction frenzy leading up to the 2022 World Cup,' *The Guardian* reported.

Qatar's appalling human rights record with regards to its migrant workers was clearly no barrier to the success of its bid either, and, while the decision is based on sporting credentials, such a catastrophic loss of lives cannot be ignored. Not only does FIFA's Executive Committee have some serious questions to answer but it also has some blood on its hands. Surely not even Blatter could turn a blind eye to such widespread and damaging abuse, but onwards they plough, seemingly oblivious to the demands of common sense and decency.

Indeed, he was prepared to travel to Qatar to find out for himself, but this fact-finding mission was postponed after the announcement of labour law reforms by the Qatari Ministry of Labour and Social Affairs. According to an official statement from FIFA, these 'confirm the expressed commitment of the country's authorities to improve the welfare of migrant workers and to use the hosting of the 2022 FIFA World Cup as a catalyst for positive social change'. Blatter tweeted, 'Pleased with news from Qatar. Big step in the right direction for sustainable change for workers' welfare.' Oh, well that's all right, then. We can all rest assured now that has been sorted.

If, by any chance, the powers that be do decide to move the World Cup to another country with an inappropriate climate, similar population, complete absence of football pedigree and piss-poor human rights record, then let's get ready for Guinea-Bissau being next in line for 2022. Or perhaps Blatter's horizons might stretch even further, so do not be surprised by a bid from Mars next time round, as long as they can sort out the air conditioning. One might imagine, after all this scandal and negative supposition, that Blatter might be a little fatigued by all the wrangling and therefore be contemplating slipping off for a quiet retirement, having previously stipulated that he would be standing down in 2015. Heaven help us as to what he will try and do next, but whatever ideas he comes up with will have to go some to match the idiocy of the Qatar 2022 decision.

R is for Rules & Regulations

> Serious sport has nothing to do with fair play. It is bound up with hatred, jealousy, boastfulness, disregard of all rules, and sadistic pleasure in witnessing violence: in other words it is war minus the shooting.
>
> From *Shooting an Elephant* by George Orwell

As we all know and accept, rules are there to be broken, and the clever, successful ones manage to break the rules without either being noticed or getting caught. All the great entertainers have been serial rule breakers. Best, Gascoigne and Cantona all earned our admiration through being close to the edge, and we were drawn to their natural ability to express themselves rather than to any inclination to conform.

Those who try to impose rules are widely regarded as killjoys, and thus referees come in for a great deal of stick and very little love. We have a natural affinity with those that cock a snook at the authorities, enjoying their frequent and inevitable run-ins. But those who are responsible for creating, implementing and enforcing the rules are not put off by this harsh treatment; indeed, it seems to spur them on to even more regulation and further confrontation with football's free spirits.

When the first rules of Association Football were introduced in 1863, there were just thirteen. Pure, plain and simple, the game benefited from not being too complicated and that is one of the primary reasons why football became so popular in Victorian Britain and soon became the national game. By being easy to understand and simple to play, football had an innate advantage over sports such as rugby.

But now the FA rulebook is a thick volume, running at a gargantuan fifty pages, with a whole host of subsections that obfuscate the simple beauty of the game. For example, the offside law, which many outsiders have never managed to understand, is now so arcane that most assistant referees have a permanently bemused look on their faces as they try to ascertain which phase a particular attack may be entering or alternatively departing. Consequently, the flag is quite often raised some time after the ball is played, and with about as much conviction as an England player taking a crucial penalty in a shoot-out.

Not only that, but also in certain matches – such as those in Europa League and Serie A – we have the dubious pleasure of six officials on duty during the games. No longer do we just have 'the man in the middle', but we also have the pair on the touchlines and a couple more behind the goals for good measure. Then there is 'the fourth official', whose main responsibility lies in mastering the digital board that signals substitutions and the amount of added time, and who tries in vain to look authoritative but is really just a glorified signpost.

The fourth official also has that uncanny ability to look away at the very point that a manager commits some horrendous indiscretion, somehow missing what everyone else has seen. There is quite an art to this form of temporary blindness, and very few are cut out for such a tricky task. This also brings us to yet another aspect of rules and regulations, which has sane men frothing at the mouth and howling at the wind – the technical area (see 'T is for Touchline').

It may sound relatively neutral and unthreatening but the technical area is a minefield of danger and deadly weapons. These rectangles of shame are now frequently host to the most heated exchanges and gladiatorial clashes, which often overshadow events on the big rectangle adjacent, otherwise known as the pitch.

Vigilance is very much on the increase, but, despite the ever-increasing number of officials and the inexorable rise of technology in dissecting the game, there are still one or two anomalies that manage to sneak past the guards. Take, for example, the taking of corners. Here the rules are plain and simple (just how we like them); the ball has to be placed in the quadrant by the corner flag. But still, the vast majority of corner kicks are taken from outside the quadrant, even when there is an assistant referee in close attendance. The strangest thing about this perpetual indiscretion is that being a few inches outside the allotted area does not provide any obvious advantage. However, players will routinely nudge the ball as if they were naughty schoolchildren making a point. Maybe the authorities should consider having four additional 'Corner Officials' to monitor this situation, and then we would have enough officials to make it to double figures, ensuring safety in numbers.

Another prime example of where the rules are flagrantly flouted is the requirement to have a defensive wall ten yards from a free kick. There is an element of theatrical orchestration surrounding this, which turns the whole affair into some form of ceremonial dance. It starts with the referee talking to those assembling to take the free kick. There is some animated conversation, and maybe even an exaggerated flourishing of the whistle to indicate that the man in charge will be blowing said whistle in the near future. Then we have *la pièce de résistance*, when the referee sets out in a very deliberate manner to march out the ten yards required. After around eight paces he usually meets the defenders, who are hoping that the ref has lost count and they can gain a few yards. But the ref is wise to this, and the wall is duly grudgingly marched back, bit by bit, to the ten-yard point.

The referee is clearly in control, and he looks terribly pleased with himself and his passable impression of the Grand Old Duke of York. Safe in the knowledge that he has done his job with a little hint of flair and panache, he now turns on his heel, ready to receive the plaudits of a grateful crowd. The sting in the tail of this accomplished manoeuvre is that once the ref has turned his back and is wallowing in the glow of self-satisfaction and mass adoration, the wall proceeds to tiptoe back to about eight yards away, as if they were a ballet troupe practising the finer points of their *pas de deux*. Subtly and surreptitiously, the wall gets back to its original mark. The entire cast in this complex dance feel as though they have come out on top in this particular battle, so it is very much a win-win situation.

Of course there has to be a great deal of sympathy for officials, who are generally waging a lonely battle against the world. Becoming a referee is not setting anyone on the path to universal popularity. For the vast majority of the time, players, managers and fans hate the ref. He is seen as biased or utterly incompetent, and usually both. However, as David Sheepshanks, former chairman of Ipswich Town and currently chairman of St George's Park, points out below in his staunch defence of the most unpopular people in football, the haranguing and hassling of referees is an unpleasant, unwelcome trait and needs to be stamped out.

David Sheepshanks, against mob rule

I hate seeing players (other than the captain) surrounding the referee after a contentious decision without being cautioned. I also hate seeing players trying to get opponents yellow carded or sent off.

I am a big supporter of our match officials, who deserve strong support. The regulations already allow for a referee to discipline players surrounding him/her. I like to see them use common sense; however, extreme examples of this ugly behaviour merit quicker punitive action, which regrettably often just does not happen at all. A few cards, yellow or even occasionally red, would soon put an end to this unruly and unsightly spectacle of 'threatening mob-type behaviour', which sets such a bad example to young players up and down the land.

I would also like to see players who try to get opponents booked or sent off when not merited in the eyes of the referee booked for ungentlemanly behaviour.

Sheepshanks' comments are his own personal view and not those of the FA or any other organisation. His first match was watching Ipswich beat Leyton Orient 3-2 on 11 April 1966 at Portman Road (the crowd was 13,352). 'I stood on the front wall near to the halfway line with three dear people, who were regular supporters and who worked for my father and offered to take me as my father had no interest at all.'

Sheepshanks is not alone in his abhorrence of the haranguing of officials, being joined by commentator Ian Darke, who currently works for BT Sport.

Ian Darke on the culture of deceit

Football is wonderful, dramatic, compulsive, intoxicating and heartbreaking – sometimes all on the same afternoon. It can also be extremely cynical. I have been hooked on the game since my father took me to Fratton Park when I was seven years old. Occasionally, Pompey players on their way home from training would join in our kick-about games in the park near the ground, and we would sprint home to tell our usually uninterested mothers.

The love affair with the game goes on, but my blood boils at football's culture of deceit. Of course, any professional sportsman or woman will get whatever edge is going, especially when the stakes are high. But a line has been crossed. The sight of players crowding round a referee waving imaginary cards, hoping to get a fellow pro booked or sent off, is repugnant.

This has become a ruthlessly calculating business, with players already on a yellow card specially targeted in an attempt to engineer a decisive eleven *v.* ten advantage.

Of course, the lawmakers should empower referees to caution these barrack-room lawyers who are forever in the ears of officials. Their attempts to influence proceedings are a disgrace to the game and an unedifying spectacle. As, incidentally, is the NFL-style blocking of goalkeepers at corners by players with no intention of playing the ball, often with their backs to the action. It must be outlawed.

My other pet hate is bookmakers laying odds on the next manager to be fired, the so-called 'Sack Race'. There are enough chairmen and owners with their fingers on the trigger without the big bookmakers giving them ideas. We are talking about a man losing his livelihood. Do we really want to be making money cashing in on another man's misfortune? I know I don't.

Having got that off my chest, it's still a great game.

Ian's first match was Portsmouth 3 Sunderland 3, while sitting on his dad's shoulders. Later, aged nineteen, he did his first live commentary for hospital radio on a Pompey game against Middlesbrough. Darke remembers being quite in awe as his co-commentator was a decent, but injured, Pompey player of the era, Harry Harris. He found out later no one heard the broadcast because of a technical fault, and according to Darke it was probably just as well.

As new regulations are churned out with increasing frequency, there are elements of the game which are buried and lost forever. When the back pass was outlawed in 1993 we said goodbye to a refined aspect of time-wasting, which involved the ball being ferried back to the goalkeeper in a continuous loop. The dominant Liverpool side of the 1970s were back pass masters, building their grip on matches with this solid foundation of keeping the ball away from the opposition and in the safe and secure hands of Ray Clemence as often as possible. Some suggested that this was a negative and stifling tactic that was encouraging sterile play, but Bill Shankly and Bob Paisley would have no doubt pointed them towards the packed trophy cabinets adorning Anfield to end any argument.

But if there is one thing that has disappeared from the game that I regret more than anything else, it is the gradual phasing out of the genuine drop ball. There was no finer sight than a fiercely contested drop ball. The suspense that built, as the ref hovered before releasing the ball in between two pumped-up protagonists, was as close as football got to the gladiatorial bravado of a bullfight. Then there was that glorious moment after the ball had bounced, when all that pent-up tension of both players was released as they competed to touch the ball first. The sheer futility of this contest was a marvel to behold as invariably whoever did manage to get in first duly proceeded to knock the ball straight to the other team. Nowadays there is a tacit agreement that one of the players will be allowed to kick the ball without anyone to challenge them as long as they return it to the opposition, which they dutifully do, accompanied by a polite round of applause for the sportsmanship on show. That is not a drop ball; that is merely a concession of possession, and we don't want it on our watch.

On the principle that it is incredibly harsh and a little unkind to kick a man while he is down, another of the worst elements of rules and regulations is the harsh practice of points being docked after a club has entered into administration. It is fair enough to punish the clubs that have transgressed the financial rules, especially as all the other clubs have had to live within their means. But for the supporters, it is often a dagger to an already broken heart. The worse thing about this cruelty is that everyone can see it coming, and there is absolutely nothing that can be done to avoid it.

The sorry trail begins with the odd rumour of financial worries circling the stricken club, and then the owners put up a distress flare calling for all involved to rally round, pleading for a serious injection of cash. The last act of this mini tragedy is played out in front of the cameras as various accountants and administrators, suited and booted and wearing troubled looks, scurry in and out of the front doors of the ground. This is when you realise the next step is that scrolling banner on the bottom of the screen as your club has so many points deducted. Rather than being on the fringes of the play-offs, the team is now two points above the drop zone and battling relegation. Dreams turn to nightmares, and all the air is sucked out of the rapidly deflating balloon.

Further angst and anguish is caused by the seemingly arbitrary nature of how many points are going to be lopped off. This ranges from three, for fielding an ineligible player, to twenty for mass indiscretions. The sliding scale has little transparency to the ordinary fan, who is now thrown headlong into the pit marked 'relegation' through no fault of his own. The final nail in the coffin is hammered home when the owners, who are primarily responsible for this financial mess, come out defiantly to start talking about a new vision for the club (See 'V is for Vision').

As they say on the street, rules are for fools and regs are for negs. We laugh in the face of authority, and revere the rule breakers – apart from the divers, the corner cheats and the card brandishers. *Vive la revolution*; let's rip up that fifty-page rule book and start all over again. For the sake of simple purity, open up Pandora's box to release the free spirit of football, demons and all, on to an expectant public.

S is for Stats

> There are three kinds of lies: lies, damned lies and statistics.
>
> Benjamin Disraeli, British Prime Minister

In the endless search for more and more content to fill the hours and hours of ever-increasing airtime, all those additional pages of newspapers and the myriad of websites dedicated to football, statistics have become a mighty weapon in the armoury of broadcasters and publishers alike. The consequent analysis rakes over every fine detail with a forensic thoroughness that leaves each match sliced and diced in numerous ways. An entire industry has sprung up to satiate the gargantuan appetite of the media for statistics. Companies have been established that focus entirely on churning out the facts and figures emanating out of every match. Data crunching has become a role as important to the clubs as physiotherapy.

There is an element of self-fulfilling prophecy involved in the whole statistics business, as one set of stats feeds off another and the whole caboodle spirals almost out of control. Whether it be possession percentages or kilometres covered, there is no wanting for information. But in the end, what does it all add up to? Pretty much a whole heap of beans, and very little else. More than any other major team sport, football is a game of ebb and flow, being dynamic and not prone to long delays in the action. Football is not suited to the level of analysis that other, more regimented and fragmented sports such as baseball and American football undergo, where the game has defined periods of play that are part of the fabric of the game. Courtesy of the likes of Opta and Prozone, and due to the work of armies of analysts, we can now wallow in 3D heat maps to our hearts' content.

The impact of Michael Lewis' 2003 book *Moneyball* revolutionised baseball, in that it unpicked the standard set of statistics and developed newer, finer ways of analysing the action. Rather than looking at generic, traditional statistics such as batting averages, Lewis went deeper into what became known as sabermetrics. By delving into more granular details such as 'slugging percentages' Lewis found a different way to evaluate players and their potential. But what worked for the Oakland A's does not necessarily mean a great deal to Leyton Orient. Such an approach cannot be transferred lock, stock and barrel to football, although many people have tried to do so, and to convince us that this key data is the solution.

Take, for example, possession statistics. These are trotted out at regular intervals during live matches, as if they were the definitive guides to determining the outcome of the match. Having the majority of possession is not a determinant to the result of a match; it never has been and it never will be. The desperate urge to show us the respective teams' share of possession as early as possible is a common feature of broadcasts. Accordingly, up pops the graphic after just ten minutes, and this then sparks a learned debate on the pattern and outcome of the match. Despite this, in seven out of ten cases a match's opening ten minutes is irrelevant to the result, and an over-reliance on stats can be self-defeating.

It has been proven in countless matches that just because a team has more possession it does not follow that this team will come out on top. Unlike the property aphorism, possession is not nine tenths of the law. It is what you do with the ball that is crucial, so once they have devised a system that analyses good possession as opposed to bad possession then they will really be on to something. The obsession with possession on its own is as useful as tracking how many times the substitutes warm up.

Pundits were left scratching their heads as to how Real could win with only a 28 per cent share of the ball after the first leg of the Real Madrid *v.* Bayern Munich 2014 Champions League semi-final at the Bernabéu, but win they did. The most extreme example of recent years involved Barcelona, when Celtic beat them in November 2012. The possession split that night was 16:84 in favour of the losers; if it had been a boxing match it would have been called off long before the end.

It is somewhat reassuring that football cannot be reduced to a series of spreadsheets, and that there remains something inherently illogical and perverse about the destiny of each match. Statistics can provide useful indicators, but they are but peripheral guides, and maybe the endless search for statistical solutions could be considered both fruitless and pointless.

Here are the thoughts of a man who should know something about statistics and their usefulness. Graham Sharpe, William Hill's Media Projects Director, has many years of experience working in sport, firstly as a journalist, and for the last forty years in a variety of roles at William Hill. The random and erroneous use of stats in commentary is one of his two specific football hates:

Stats in commentary – Graham Sharpe, William Hill

The first is – are – irritating commentators which, I admit, is a very personal bugbear, but there is nothing worse than sitting down to watch a match, wishing just to be informed of who has the ball and is passing to which player, together with informed interjections from an expert analyst, only to be bombarded with incessant, superfluous nonsense.

Far too frequently, we end up having to listen to a verbally incontinent egotist spouting a plethora of pre-prepared irrelevant stats and opinions which he (almost exclusively) will insist on inserting in to his commentary, absolutely regardless of whether or not they 'fit' with what is going on in the game. My own name for this commentator condition is Tyler-Drury disease, but you may have your own descriptive appellation.

My second dislike is the way in which, these days, the stats with which so many commentators and pundits are apparently obsessed are granted an almost mystic respect to which they are by no means entitled.

As we all know, it is possible to 'prove' any theory or belief by judicious use of selective stats. But if what has gone before in different circumstances and at a different time had any genuine relevance to what was about to happen, then the bookmaking profession would have ceased to exist by now.

Who cares that every time these teams have met over the past thirty-seven years both sides have scored, or that player 'x' has scored against this team every time they meet when there is an 'R' in the month? I most certainly do not, nor do I wish to be told such banal, unimportant, useless drivel.

Graham supports Luton Town, and the very first match he went to was at local amateur club Wealdstone, who were, coincidentally, responsible for both Stuart Pearce and Vinnie Jones. His first professional game was Fulham *v.* Blackpool in around 1962.

S is for Stepovers

That's one small step for a man, one giant leap for mankind.

Neil Armstrong, astronaut, on landing on the moon

Skill attracts us to the game, and consequently skilful players are treated like minor deities as they unveil their box of tricks with pace and panache. The sight of a tricky winger bamboozling a hapless defender is one of the most wonderful aspects of the game. Yet there is one skill in the armoury that gets the blood boiling and causes minor apoplexy every time it is unleashed. The stepover itself is fine in isolation as it is a simple move, one that unbalances the opponent; the problem lies in the multiple, repetitive use, which causes no end of bother.

The man who is generally considered to have introduced the stepover to Europe was, almost inevitably, a Dutchman. Although Law Adam sounds like a deputy sheriff from the American Midwest, he was actually a footballer in the 1920s and 1930s who plied his trade for Den Haag in the Netherlands and Grasshopper Zürich in Switzerland. Apparently adopted from the scissors manoeuvre employed by figure skaters, Adam developed a reputation as a skilful and tricky opponent after perfecting the art of the stepover. Many Dutch exponents of the art followed, and the move later became a favourite of Brazilians, with Ronaldo and Denílson becoming well known for their silky interpretations.

The man who has moved the manoeuvre on to a new level is Cristiano Ronaldo, and it is that new level which can so infuriate. He is not content to do it once, but repeats the dose to the point at which we cry 'no more'. It goes beyond the purpose of beating a man and actually ends up humiliating him. It is excessive, it is demeaning, and it is plain wrong. Outwitting a man is fine, but doing it repeatedly to the point of distraction is sadistic and unpleasant. This is no longer a tactic to overcome an opponent, but more a weapon of mass destruction that often leaves the tormented defender confused and angry. Once or twice is acceptable, but after you get past three there is no practical purpose apart from blatant exhibitionism. There is also the trace of a sadistic sneer that creeps across Ronaldo's face when he is inflicting such pain. His stepovers are a study in ostentation and oppression, ugly and cruel in a similar way to a pastime popular in his adopted country, bullfighting.

The teasing is reminiscent of one of my early experiences of Sunday morning football in south-east London, when I tried to play my way out of a tight defensive spot by dribbling it past a couple of forwards before passing the ball out wide. Having accomplished this, I was feeling quite proud of myself, when out of nowhere I was crunched by a clearly disgruntled, outraged opponent while the ball was way off in the distance. When challenged about his unnecessary, off-the-ball challenge, his response could be summed up as 'please do not try anything fancy, your job is to hoof the ball out and anything else is an insult to me and my fellow forwards, and we will dole out the requisite punishment for such audaciousness'. The message was delivered in not so many words, however, but rather in a few strong expletives.

What this man of Woolwich would have made of Ronaldo's befuddling stopovers goodness only knows, but it would have been neither pretty nor clever. Nevertheless, his response might just have stopped the mercurial Portuguese in his tracks and made him think twice about indulging in his habit of humiliating his hapless opponent.

T is for Touchlines

> The field of play must be rectangular and marked with lines. These lines belong to the areas of which they are boundaries.
>
> The two longer boundary lines are called touchlines. The two shorter lines are called goal lines.
>
> From 'FIFA Laws of the Game – Field Markings'

It all seems so straightforward, in that we have touchlines and goal lines; but that is not the half of it, and underneath lurks a monster. Touchlines may have started out on the periphery of the action, but they have grown in significance at every level of football and have increasingly become the centre of attention. Touchlines are a source of angst and uncontrollable anger, and are home to some of the most spiteful acts in football. They are a seething cauldron of distemper and dystopia that now resembles a WWE contest rather than a place for cool, calm, rational thinking. Something happens to people as they hover around the touchline that turns them into subhuman life forms. It is as if they have entered a new, lawless world.

Take Alan Pardew; he generally conducts himself with self-control and restraint in all walks of life, but get him near a touchline and he is like a man possessed, raging and ranting to anyone within touching distance. When he was the manager at West Ham, Pardew had a couple of feisty spats with Wenger, and then turned physical at Newcastle by pushing an assistant referee, before returning to a torrent of verbal abuse against Pelligrini. Finally, and infamously, he lost his head in a contretemps with David Meyler of Hull City that resembled a pair of rutting stags getting close and personal.

6. The flashpoint between Hull's David Meyler and Newcastle manager Alan Pardew brought new meaning to the phrase 'use your head, son'.

This unsavoury incident prompted a review of the technical areas, which have become the battlegrounds for a host of hotheads. It as if the touchline has become the blue touchpaper, ready to be ignited at the slightest provocation. In light of Pardew's headstrong action, Richard Bevan, Chief Executive of the League Managers Association, was forced to make a statement on the tricky and sensitive subject. The solution lay not in asking managers such as Pardew to control themselves, but in removing the temptation of confrontation by relocating the technical areas themselves, as if they were the problem. There was no word of censure to the manager who had pushed his head into the face of a player.

'It shows you the extreme stress of the job,' Bevan said, 'even when you are in a winning position. The League Managers Association is here to support managers and we'll be talking about areas that we are reviewing.

'We are currently researching with a university into how the technical area operates.

'We did a technical report six or seven months ago – we interviewed forty referees and managers – looking at the behaviour, the position, the objective of the technical area, and comparing it with other sports, for example in the United States, to see how we can improve several problems that occur because of its positioning.'

There is so much posturing going on by managers that what was the sideshow has become the main attraction. Tim Sherwood's flouncing, gilet-throwing hissy fits created the headlines, while the performance – and even the result – is almost incidental to the main story. Pretty soon the betting firms will be offering odds on which minute terrible Tim will be discarding his first piece of clothing, or how far he will chuck his sleeveless jacket. Aside from the coat chucking, managerial hand gesticulations have now reached such a level that it would be no surprise to see some explanatory notes in the programme. There are so many permutations that it has got to the point where players need a BA in semaphore to understand the instructions. Less tiki-taka, more tic-tac. Maybe this newfound skill set is relaying the in-play odds of the next yellow card (see 'G is for Gambling').

One of the original touchline terrors was that of Eric Cantona, following his robust response to being abused by a fan at Selhurst Park in January 1995. Cantona certainly crossed the line while being escorted to the dressing rooms, after being sent off, by jumping into the stands and aiming a kung fu kick and a flurry of punches at his *bête noire*. Subsequently banned from playing for six months, the *enfant terrible* cemented his reputation for being a dangerous mixture of talent and trouble, and created a dangerous precedent for touchline tantrums.

Quite possibly the most unedifying and disturbing aspect of touchline misbehaviour takes place a long way from the glare and glamour of the Premier League. Across every park in the country and throughout thousands of leagues there lurks the darkest, most malign of influences

– the touchline dads. Perfectly decent, respectable human beings undergo a scarcely credible dehumanising process, as these ordinary people become monsters. The transformation happens in an instant; blink and you will miss it. One minute the touchline dad will be discussing the finer points of government policy on social inclusion, and the next he will be leaping into the air with spit drooling down his jowls, castigating the referee for his lack of control and turning the air blue with the most vehement vitriol.

Matt Dickinson, chief sports correspondent of *The Times*, has seen this sort of terrifying mutation up close. He has been taken aback by the sheer ferocity of the venom, and shocked by how it comes out of nowhere. Even in the leafy, genteel surroundings of south-west London the touchline dad is alive and kicking (every ball), as Dickinson reveals from his own experience of watching his son perform for Under-10s in the local youth league. Although this may not sound like a hotbed of football, there is certainly enough heat generated by those touchline dads to fuel a small power station.

Matt Dickinson on touchline dads

A nine-year-old girl is uncertainly practising her violin at home when, mid-piece, her father walks up and screams, 'PUT SOME ELBOW INTO IT!' As a twelve-year-old boy hesitates over his maths homework, his mother shouts at him to 'GET STUCK IN!' Those examples seem not just absurd but self-defeating, hindering performance (not to mention enjoyment) by creating unnecessary stress around what should be a fun learning experience. Yet that is exactly what we do with our budding young footballers on Saturday and Sunday mornings.

You see it on every park pitch, every weekend. We stand on the side and inflict a din on their ears. Even if those shouts are well-intentioned, they are just a wall of noise to a young boy or girl who is trying to explore their way in the game, hoping to find the courage and confidence to try something different.

English football is famous for the passion of its supporters, but we seem unable to distinguish between the right outlet and heckling our own children. A friend who moved to Spain told me that the first thing he noticed was not that every young kid could pass like Xavi, but that, as the children played, the Dads would sit sipping coffees and watch from a distance.

We shout and holler from the touchline, and it drives me crackers. It makes players afraid to be daring, it over-emphasises the importance of the result among children, and, more often than not, the noise has nothing to do with encouraging creative skill.

It is why, as the FA holds a grand Commission to discover why we produce so few English players and the Premier League pours hundreds of millions into new academies, I would start with one very simple rule right down at the bottom, which can help to transform our football culture at a stroke. I would ban all parents from saying a word. They would be permitted to ask just one question – 'was that fun?' – and only after the final whistle.

Dickinson is a Cambridge United fan, whose first match was Leeds *v.* Bristol City in November 1979.

T is for Throw-Ins

It's like a human sling.

David Moyes, then Everton manager, on Rory Delap in 2008

People scoff at the rather blunt weapon that is the long throw-in. It is a tactic that is anathema to most who appreciate the finer things in life, being a show of brute strength as opposed to a sublime skill. Although there is a close association between Stoke and the art of the long throw-in, the first exponent was not Rory Delap but a cultured inside forward. The late Ian Hutchinson played a pivotal part in Chelsea's FA Cup victory in the 1970 replay against Leeds, setting up the winning goal for Dave Webb with one of his speciality throws which propelled the ball to the far post, flummoxing the likes of Jackie Charlton and Norman Hunter. The windmill action Hutchinson developed became his trademark, and following his death in 2002 most obituaries referred to his throw-ins rather than any of his other footballing abilities.

While it is an impressive technique to be able to hurl the ball over fifty metres, there is still a part of us that bemoans its use. This is maybe because there is no relation to the feet, which, after all, are the essential tools of the game. It feels like more of a circus act than a skill that would have been honed on the training grounds of Barcelona or Bayern Munich. Aside from the aesthetic argument, there was also an element of subterfuge and gamesmanship. When ball boys (See 'B is for Ball Boys') are instructed to provide towels to dry the ball, but solely for the home side's use, and advertising hoardings are conveniently parted to allow a decent run-up, then we are veering into not just gaining an advantage but also plain old-fashioned cheating. This is football's equivalent of cricket's great sin of ball tampering, and it should not be encouraged.

Back in the late 1990s, there was even a contest to judge whose throw was the longest. Dave Challinor of Tranmere Rovers became the unofficial world-record holder, when he overcame the inappropriately named Andy Legg of Cardiff with a prodigious throw of just under fifty metres. That a separate contest was held suggests that this was a distinct event, something that could have become a new Olympic sport, perhaps, but it does not fit in with the ebb and flow that lies at the heart of the game of football. It veers close to the 'special teams' employed in American football, and needs to be resisted if muscularity is not to overtake and ruin the sport as a spectacle.

The long throw-in belongs in the same camp as those coaches who urge players 'to get it in the mixer', or subscribe to the Charles Hughes 'direct football' philosophy, which dictated that five passes was the optimum number in any one move. If all we wanted from football was plain, unadulterated efficiency, then this would suffice, but ultimately we yearn for a more refined approach and something less utilitarian.

U is for U-Turns

> To those waiting with bated breath for that favourite media catchphrase, the U-turn, I have only one thing to say. You turn if you want to. This lady's not for turning.
>
> Margaret Thatcher, UK Prime Minister

Football folk are a fickle bunch, swaying this way and that to court public opinion. The preponderance of U-turns that have been liberally sprinkled across the years is clear evidence of how capricious football can be. So whether it is the manager who decides not to retire after all, or the player who would never play for a certain club but then eventually does after a juicy contract is waved in front of his nose, there is a plethora of abrupt changes of heart. In the end, we should not be surprised by any of these switches in allegiance or changes in commitment; the U-turn is as much part of the game as the dribble or the pass. The screeching of tyres is such a regular backdrop to so many of the big, bold statements that are trotted out time and again that it is more of a surprise that people still believe most of the stuff that is churned out. In the future, these proclamations are best taken with a huge, industrial dose of salt, as our cynical distrust of most statements grows apace.

One of the best-known U-turns was executed by Sir Alex Ferguson, the man who has cast his lengthy shadow over English football over the last quarter of a century. For someone who developed a fearsome reputation, and indeed built much of his formidable career around sticking stubbornly to his guns, it is ironic that he should perform one of the most significant reversals. When Ferguson announced his retirement in 2002, it was the passing of an era, football's equivalent of a JFK moment. Thousands of words were written on his contribution in transforming Manchester United into the dominant club of the last decade or so, as the epitaphs and tributes flowed. But, in the end, Ferguson was not content to walk away, and he backtracked from his original decision. Eleven years later, with six more Premier League titles and another Champions League trophy added, he finally relinquished the reins at Old Trafford.

However, considering the difficulties his successor, David Moyes, encountered in his first season, there were some who suggested that another U-turn was in the offing. Clearly, Ferguson found it difficult to depart from the stage, and each United defeat under Moyes was accompanied by images of the Scot bristling with exasperation in the stands. He had been hovering in the wings like a retired actor unwilling to say his last goodbye to his adoring audience. Despite all the protestations to the contrary, there was surely a small, shrill voice on his shoulder entreating him to make yet another comeback. The spectre of the next U-turn was still very much alive, haunting Moyes until he was shuffled out of Old Trafford less than a year after his arrival as the Chosen One.

One of Ferguson's closest rivals was not averse to some U-turn chicanery himself. Jose Mourinho's departure from Chelsea in 2007 was a messy affair, with bridges not so much burned as incinerated. Mourinho and Abramovich fell out, and there seemed no way back as Jose headed off initially to Inter Milan and then Madrid. But back he came in 2013, and they kissed and made up, with Mourinho insisting that there was never a problem between the two and that that they had decided to go their separate ways for a while. Does he really expect us to believe such errant nonsense and sweep everything under the carpet? Of course, people can change their minds and have every right to do so, but please do not insult our intelligence by pretending that nothing was amiss.

The same can be said for players who are itching for a new club, attracting suitors left, right and centre, before undergoing their very own Damascene conversion as their existing club coughs up an improved offer. The sudden change of heart is then portrayed as further evidence of their undying loyalty and love of the club. Wayne Rooney has been through this very process on a few occasions. In 2013 he coquettishly fluttered his eyelashes at Chelsea, and Mourinho started to get excited about a potential move before Rooney landed a hefty wage increase, the biggest long-term contract in United's history. Rooney stayed put, insisting that he had never wanted to leave in the first place. This merry dance is repeated up and down the land, but nearly always ends up in the same place.

Alongside the frequent transfer turnarounds, there is an exhaustive list of players who retire gracefully, only to return to the fray within the space of a few months. Having grown quickly disillusioned with the prospect of endless rounds of golf, long afternoons playing *FIFA 2014* or coaching in the Vietnamese First Division, they renege on the deal to hang up their boots. They are supposedly coaxed out of retirement, but the haste at which they return to the fray is indicative of someone who has had those boots ready for several weeks. Miraculously, they appear at the training ground within seconds of the announcement being made, faster than you can say, 'I am fit and more than ready to do a job for the team, even though I am older than the manager.'

U is for Ultra

Basta larne, basta infami.
('Cut out the knives, cut out the infamy.')

From Bergamo ultra

The development of the ultra movement in Italian football during the 1960s and 1970s has been well chronicled. The curious mixture of political extremism, regional rivalry and ostentatious displays, all served up with an undercurrent of violence, has marred *calcio* for many years. That all the major clubs allowed, nay encouraged, such behaviour is an indication of how rotten Italian football had become even before the high-profile scandals of Totonero or Calciopoli came to light. In fact, it reached such a level that some clubs would be effectively run by the ultra, who had became omnipotent. It reached a stage when the ultra even started to determine the selection of the team, with the threat of retribution hanging over a manager who dared to go against their wishes.

There are many traits of the ultra's ethos that are deeply unpleasant – the political extremism, the violence, the corruption – but perhaps the single most irksome thing that they have brought into football stadiums is the megaphone. The use of a megaphone by the leaders of the ultra, or *capo curva*, to whip up the fans' frenzy is akin to dropping a lighted match on to a pool of petrol. The rasping noise is an unbearable distraction during the match, and the artificiality of having to project the chanting through an amplifier exposes the ultra for the sham that they are. It is, alongside the idea of piping crowd noise to add to the atmosphere, a heinous crime. They are not so much football fans as meddlesome individuals, determined and duly organised to cause the maximum amount of trouble. Some of their antics, such as throwing scooters from one tier to another, are dubious to say the least.

John Foot, author of *Calcio*, the definitive history of Italian football, goes even further in his condemnation of the ultra and he has had enough of their egotism.

The curse of the ultra – John Foot

Once upon a time, I thought it was all quite exciting. The flares, the orchestrated singing, the banners, the extremist politics and the violence before, during and after the game. But now, after twenty-five years of watching Italian football, I am bored to tears by it all. The ultra are organised fans who control stadiums in many countries, but they are perhaps at their strongest in Italy. Every week, they turn up very early for games, preparing their massive banners with obscure messages usually aimed at the press or other ultra. Some of them become 'ultra-chief', and they sit or stand at the front, facing the others, telling them what and when to sing. If you are unlucky enough to get a ticket among the ultra, they will spot you straight away, and you will have to do what they tell you to. Their songs are often boring and repetitive. Their politics are usually right-wing (nowadays, at least), and often downright fascist and racist. They bicker among themselves and fight for position on the *curva* (an area of the ground – each and every ground – they control) with other groups. The ultra are only interested in one thing – themselves. They don't really care about football. They don't even watch the game half the time. They just want to get their message across, whatever that message might be, and it's usually a message about themselves. Disagree with them? You might get hurt. Try and challenge their 'right' to display insulting banners or throw flares? You might need an armed guard. The press salivates over their every message and statement, frequently calling them 'the fans' (and thus ignoring the 99.9 per cent of fans who are not 'ultra'). And then there is the 'ultra mentality', which involves edicts on how to stab people without killing them (in the buttocks is apparently a very good way of doing this) and mumbo-jumbo about 'honour', 'spies', 'the state', 'modern football' and so on ad nauseam. Once part of what made Italian football particularly interesting, the ultra are now very much part of the problem. Delusional and achingly dull, they continue to act as if nothing has changed in the world, standing there shouting out a series of repetitive and non-ironic chants, game after game,

> day after day. Enough, already. You have had your time. Basta!

John is an Arsenal fan, whose first match was Tottenham *v.* Manchester City in around 1972 with his dad, the renowned journalist Paul Foot. 'Rodney Marsh was playing. That's all I really remember, plus the overwhelming smell of cigarettes and urine and the view of a man's bottom in front of me.' No wonder he found Italian football so attractive, at least initially.

What the ultra have in common with many of the figures of hate featured in this book is that their motivation is primarily selfish. As Foot points out, football is treated as an effective means of expressing their opinions, rather than the end in itself. One has to be deeply suspicious of people who use football's popularity as leverage to promote their own views. It is an exercise in callous cynicism that has no place among the legions of genuine fans whose love of football is pure, untainted by any other consideration than passion for the game.

V is for Vision

For the vision of one man lends not its wings to another man.

From *The Prophet* by Kahlil Gibran

When someone starts postulating about their vision for the club, it is time to man the lifeboats and start donning the life jacket, because the next step is oblivion. It is especially worrying if the person claiming to have vision is the chairman, as this basically signifies the end of the club as we know it. Just take Portsmouth. Everything was rosy in the garden in 2008; they had just won the FA Cup for the first time in over seventy years, were happily ensconced in the middle of the Premier League, and the chairman, Alex Gaydamak, was one of the new tranche of foreign owners with a bottomless pit of cash, or so everyone was led to believe. A new squad had been assembled under Harry Redknapp, and all was going swimmingly. Then disaster struck, as talk of building a new stadium to replace the quaint but creaking Fratton Park was rife under the banner of Pompey's stunning stadium *vision*.

Once the V word had been used, the whole charade unpicked itself quicker than Auntie Jean's Christmas jumper. Within a year, the club had gone into administration for the first time, but not for the last. The chairman departed, leaving the club in the clutches of a disparate bunch of desperadoes, and in between the two spells of administration there was just enough time to squeeze in three relegations. Facing life in League Two, the club fell into the open arms of the fans under the guise of the Pompey Supporters Trust, with, by a strange twist of fate, good old Fratton Park a key component in the rescue plan. So much for the stunning stadium vision of five years earlier, which had disappeared as quickly as Portsmouth had tumbled down the League.

Portsmouth finished the 2013/14 season in their lowest League position for over a century. But the curse of the vision syndrome does not just affect those at the bottom of the League pyramid, as Manchester United fans will testify. David Moyes' uncomfortable inheritance post-Ferguson was never going to be a smooth transition, but a faltering League campaign, with losses in double figures – including a couple of humiliating 3-0 hammerings at home to arch rivals Liverpool and City – made it almost unbearable for United fans. Following the first of those tonkings at Old Trafford, Moyes talked about his relationship with the board and owners. 'That is why they gave me a six-year contract, because this is not a club that works on a short-term vision; it works on a long-term vision,' Moyes reassured us. And with that fateful mention of vision, the die was cast.

Within a couple of months, that long-term vision went up in smoke and Moyes was on his way, being shown the door after ten inglorious months in charge. Some deemed this a harsh, hasty and brutal move, but as soon as the dreaded vision genie was out of the bottle there was only one direction the Moyes era was heading. Vision is a deadly virus, and as soon as it is spotted it needs to be eradicated, otherwise the damage will be long lasting and probably irreparable. A meltdown of gruesome proportions will be in the offing from this one poisonous source, especially when it starts from the very top.

There is also the contamination that affects the players as well as the chairman and manager. Once a footballer is described as having 'great vision', his fate is sealed, and there is no turning back. This is a euphemism for his knees are knackered, his pace has gone and all he has left are his eyes, and they are not as strong as they used to be. Michael Carrick is an example of such a player, continuously talked about as having vision, which means he can no longer really cut it physically; he can see it but he just cannot do it. Regularly, commentators will say that he can see a pass. After so many years as a professional footballer it would be rather odd if he could not see a pass.

The most perturbing football vision, which caused the deepest disquiet, was courtesy of one Daniel Geller. Daniel's father Uri, the psychic who built his reputation on bending spoons, was inspired to take over Exeter City on the back of a dream that his twenty-one-year-old son had had about the collective hanging of witches in the local area. Naturally, Geller's next move was to install himself as chairman of the football club and embark on Exeter's long climb out of the bottom division, but the grand plan did not quite take off. Despite enlisting the help of Michael Jackson and David Blaine in June 2002 to bring the plight of the Grecians to a global audience, the rescue never materialised.

Geller's vision lasted for just over a year, until Exeter did indeed leave the fourth tier of English football after being relegated to the Conference, one of the first clubs to do so as part of the two-up two-down system implemented that season. His evident disappointment was expressed as an unwanted vision. 'I'm wishing it was a nightmare and that I'd wake up but, of course, it's not,' Geller wailed. But that is the problem with visions in football. They do often turn into nightmares, and no amount of cutlery-bending psychic powers or celebrity appearances can break the spell. As the vision receded, Geller rid himself of this turbulent football club and the sorry saga drew to a close. If Geller cannot rectify the situation, then we have reached the land of the last resort and are cast adrift in the sea of oblivion, much as Exeter were back in 2003.

The last thing that anyone needs when their backs are up against the wall is to hear the dreaded word 'vision'. It is pretty much the death knell, and is time for all concerned to admit defeat and start making preparations for a season or two in the doldrums, whether it is Exeter, Portsmouth or Manchester United involved. Irrespective of the history or pedigree of the club, the result is the same slippery slide.

V is for Victory Parades

In defeat unbeatable; in victory unbearable.

Winston Churchill

Victory can be so sweet, and, as fans, we savour that moment – especially if it is either unexpected or significant, and all the better if it is both. It is what we yearn for, and the main aim of the game. However, there is something about a victory parade that is really disturbing. Do we really need to line the streets to catch a glimpse of our heroes cavorting in an open-top bus? Also what happens to these open-top buses in the intervening period, which can stretch over many years? Do they end up in a desert like so many abandoned aeroplanes? The justification is that this is an opportunity to celebrate together, but surely this has already been done at the matches themselves. Of the thousands present, how many are true fans? Or are they glory hunters merely jumping on the bandwagon of success?

The victory parade verges into gloating territory, and there has to be serious questioning of whether this is strictly necessary. The one thing that is guaranteed is that if there is a trophy involved it will be dropped, dented or damaged in some way. It is all part of merry japes, all done in the spontaneous outburst of joy, and it seems just a little bit disrespectful. The team have fought tooth and nail to win the trophy and then they fling it around with reckless abandon, and it is all a little too contrived and pre-meditated for my liking. It can also be wholly inappropriate; for example, celebrating being runners-up or losing finalists with a civic reception at the town hall is surely a bus trip too far.

It is also the timing of these parades that raises cause for concern. They have been planned well in advance, in some cases too early, and have to be hastily abandoned when the team fail to deliver. The fact that the parades take place many days after the event means they can hardly be looked at as a natural outburst of positive vibes. And there is also just too much smiling and waving going on for my liking. Added to which, the wrong sort of fans (see 'P is for Plastics') are drawn towards this vainglorious exhibition so they can show off all the crappiest paraphernalia in their locker. The worst is very much in evidence all the way along the route, from the obligatory jesters' hats to awful foam hands, from tatty plastic flags to ghastly painted faces. It is a shocking sight that brings dishonour to all involved, and it really is time to call a halt to victory parades for once and for all. To the victor, the spoiled.

W is for Wave (Mexican)

> An effect like a moving wave produced by sections of a stadium crowd standing and sitting down again one after the other while raising and lowering their arms.
>
> *Oxford English Dictionary* definition

If there were ever a tainted legacy from a World Cup tournament, it would have to be from Mexico 1986. While it was not the infamous Hand of God, nor yet those ill-fitting blue England shorts, this was still in so many ways the most reprehensible act amid a whole catalogue of appalling incidents. The main reason why this one stands out from the rest is that this has since been played out on countless occasions, whereas the other misdemeanours were one-offs, and have fortunately never been repeated.

The origins of the Mexican wave are hotly disputed, with various claims as to who was responsible, but the blame seems to lie squarely with one of the big four American sports. The first appearance cast its ignominious shadow in the 1970s, at either a baseball game or an American

combination that has successfully replaced the sterility and negativity of previous tournaments. There have been very few dull matches. Even those that have not shown much spark have been transformed by a flurry of excitement towards the end, such as the Argentina–Switzerland game, which exploded into life in the last few minutes.

There has been the successful and sensible introduction of the referees' magic spray to mark out the requisite ten yards at free kicks. Such a simple and effective idea may well be FIFA's finest hour. We have even been saved the torture of English hubris; the team managed to live down to low expectations and lasted just over a week, allowing us to enjoy the tournament with dispassionate objectivity. The (admittedly hugely expensive) gleaming stadiums have been impressive and, more importantly, nearly all have been close to full capacity. The atmosphere for the majority of games has been exceptionally vibrant, but there was a blot on the copybook and one that cannot be ignored.

It has happened in every match, regardless of the state of the game, and it is a crying shame that has taken the gloss off the festival of football that all of us have been enjoying. It is deplorable and inexcusable for a genuine football nation such as Brazil to have allowed this to happen. There does not even have to be a lull in the pace of the action on the pitch for it to start, and once it has begun its inexorable surge we are forced to endure a few minutes of its ghastly, all-consuming trajectory. In 2014 the Mexican wave is, much to everyone's chagrin, still alive.

W is for World Cup Draw

I hope they let me back in the country!

Sir Geoff Hurst after the World Cup draw in Brazil

For such a prestigious and much-revered tournament, it is a pity that the preamble is such a shambles. To string out the relatively straightforward process of organising thirty-two teams into eight groups, turning it into an extravaganza of balls and b-list celebrities, is an extraordinary exercise in procrastination and obfuscation. A task that should take a twelve-year-old with an average mathematical aptitude around fifteen minutes to complete is somehow transformed into a tortuous two-and-a-half-hour marathon. The time is mainly filled with the wheeling out of as many former players as it is possible to cram on to one stage. The old stars appear alongside the obligatory local children, who look ever so slightly lost, dazed and confused at having been dragged into this farrago.

Flying in a gaggle of former players from every corner of the globe for their fifteen seconds of fame as they unveil the contents of Pot C could be regarded as a monumental waste of time. But so what if the carbon footprint is compromised? There is a pressing need to fly Geoff Hurst halfway around the world for this rigmarole. Nevertheless, the cost of all those essential flights is dwarfed by the construction bill of over-elaborate sets that look better suited to staging the latest leg of Madonna on tour. No expense is spared, but this does not guarantee a smooth-running, successful operation.

The 1982 draw from Madrid will go down in the annals as the most hopeless endeavour, swimming on a flotsam of cash and jetsam of utter incompetence. It was a veritable hotchpotch of spinning cages that stopped spinning and exploding balls spilling their contents, and even featured a redraw, after a flawed start that saw Belgium and Scotland somehow drawn in the wrong groups. The whistling of the audience as the ceremony limped from one disaster to another was acutely embarrassing for all FIFA officials, including a fresh-faced but clearly perturbed general secretary, whose baptism presiding over the first draw to be televised live could hardly have gone worse.

Adding grist to the mill, this massive balls-up cost almost $9 million to stage. At least, by setting the bar so low, it has made all subsequent draws look vaguely competent and models of efficiency by comparison. This did not hold back the irresistible rise of the poor unfortunate presiding officer, whose fledgling career could have been scuppered by it all. But since this utter debacle, which would have surely ruined lesser men, he has gone on from strength to strength, reaching the top job as president for eighteen years. Oh, Mr Blatter, how the fallen are so mighty.

The draw for the 2014 tournament was less flamboyant than the 1982 effort, but, for England, it displayed our unfailing capacity to shoot ourselves in the foot long before the action has begun. When Roy Hodgson described Manaus, the venue for their opening match against Italy, as the 'place to avoid' he did not exactly enamour Team England to the locals. The mayor, Arthur Virgilio, was not that keen to roll out the red carpet on hearing this slight on his town, declaring that 'we would also prefer that England doesn't come. We hope to get a better team and a coach who is more sensible and polite.' There is nothing like getting the locals fully behind your team, but unfortunately, this proved to be nothing like it.

In addition to Hodgson's ill-chosen words, FA chairman Greg Dyke unveiled his 'cut throat' gesture in response to the team's chances after drawing a tough group, and so the obituaries were being readied a full six months before we had even kicked a ball in anger. With these two consummate diplomats responsible for heading up England's campaign to defy the odds and restore some sort of credibility to our latest foray into World Cup history, what could possibly go wrong? Who needs bored players venting their frustration, or giggling WAGs cavorting on shopping trips, to derail our best intentions when we have the Roy and Greg show rolling into town?

The charade that is the World Cup draw could be swept away and consigned to its rightful place in the dustbin marked 'colossal waste of time and resources' if FIFA finally cut to the chase and made the whole qualification process much more transparent. My notion is that, in the future, countries need not go through the rather convoluted and antiquated qualification process. Let's rid ourselves of this irksome practice and base participation on the only sensible criteria: wealth. I propose that, from now on, the thirty-two nations with the highest gross domestic product in the year before the World Cup will be pitted against each other, thereby ensuring a rosy financial future. The added benefit is that seeding and group composition can be based on this readily available data, and we could have some anonymous IMF bureaucrat to do the donkeywork. No fuss, no bother and as clean as a whistle.

X is for Xenophobia

> The intense or irrational dislike or fear of people from other countries.
>
> Definition of 'xenophobia' from *The Concise Oxford Dictionary*

Xenophobia is still very much apparent in today's football world, and although racism is not nearly as rife as it was back in the dark days of the 1970s and 1980s, it still lurks, casting a shadow over the game. Despite the massive influx of talent from across the globe – the Premier League has featured players from over 100 countries and counting – fear and distrust still exists in large pockets of the football firmament.

It starts so surreptitiously with the odd quip about the essential differences between the English mentality and those of other countries. What is hinted at is that we, the English, have a natural, innate superiority in that we have that essential ingredient of spirit. Not skill, not tactical genius, not anything refined but an indomitable attitude, which means we will never give up, even in the face of adversity. Accepting that everyone else is more adept and ahead of us is all part and parcel of being the pluckiest of losers.

But then there is a change in mood, just as England are heading for their traditional early exit; accusations of nefarious activities emerge, and we are into full on blame game. Paolo Hewitt describes the difference between an England player 'going to ground' and a pesky foreigner who seeks to gain an unfair advantage, or, to put it another way, is blatantly cheating.

Paolo Hewitt – racism

Then there is the racism. If a foreign player dives, it is an ineradicable stain on the beautiful game, a filthy dirty rotten trick, typical of the country in question. Yet if an England player dives (Owen against Argentina), it is either ignored (Sheringham *v.* Greece), or relayed as the player in question showing guile, being a bit cheeky eh chaps, wink wink?

I was in Italy just after that great country's 2006 triumph. A friend of my relatives collared me. 'You live in London, right? When you get back to England tell those English this: Italy has won the World Cup four times and the English have only won it once. And when they did, they cheated!

Messrs Pearce and Townsend, you have been duly served.

When Ronaldo winked after Rooney's dismissal during the World Cup quarter final in 2006, the nation was up in arms. How dare he revel in our man's misfortune, we raged, and it emboldened the view that it was us against the rest of the world. It confirmed, once and for all, that we were being conned out of our natural inheritance by those pesky Portuguese. Facing a world that is packed with dissemblers who are out to trick our brave boys out of the tournament, what chance have we got? Forget the massive gulf in coaching techniques and grass roots investment to which most other major footballing countries have been wedded for years; it is all a dastardly plot and it is most unfair.

Take the catastrophe that was Bloemfontein in 2010, when Frank Lampard's strike at the end of the first half did not so much cross the line as ripple the back of the net, undetected by the match officials. It was clearly a conspiracy, and the fact that England had been completely outplayed by Germany – a trend that continued in the second half – was conveniently brushed aside by the tide of moral indignation unleashed towards FIFA and anyone else in the vicinity. Yet again, left with just a righteous sense of moral superiority, we limp away to lick our wounds for another four years. The blame game very rarely focuses on our own shortcomings, but concentrates on the scheming of others from further afield.

There is a pervading sense that we English suffer from being too honest for our own good. If only we could allow ourselves to do a deal with the devil, then we would be so much more successful. In the end, we will stick to our principles and hang the consequences, safe in the knowledge that we may not be close to winning anything but at least we have the moral high ground, which nobody can take away from us. Our traditional method of going out on penalties is treated as though we have been denied by some malevolent spirit. How dare the Germans be so ruthlessly efficient at spot kicks, we bleat, and, rumour has it, they even admit to practice taking them. We would never stoop that low in pursuit of victory. After all, it is much better to be plucky losers as opposed to scheming winners.

It is not just the national team that suffers from such a warped view of the world. Our brave boys are also often denied in European club competitions. While the opposition resort to appalling time-wasting, we indulge in controlling the game with intelligence. Our players show commitment and passion while theirs are over-excitable and dirty. Probably the most glaringly obvious comparison is the way we tackle, which is with honest gusto, while they are sneaky and underhand and of course the foreign referees do not understand the difference, so we get punished unduly. When an opposition player is hacked down and our man is sent off, the standard line is trotted out that this sort of robust challenge would not even merit a free kick, let alone a card, in the Premier League. We are made of sterner stuff than the flimsy French or the soppy Spanish. It is all so terribly unfair to have good old Blighty blighted.

X is for Ex-Factor

I'll be revenged on the whole pack of you.
From *Twelfth Night* by William Shakespeare

There is one immutable law in football, and it is one that comes to haunt us all too often. It runs like this: whenever a former player returns to play against your own team, you can bet your bottom dollar that he will score. Selling him, however, was an easy decision, given that he had never showed the slightest inclination of running into any vein of form, rich or otherwise, during his time with your team. Once ushered out of the door, there is not a murmur of resistance or regret because he fails to make an impact elsewhere. The doubts only start creeping in with the realisation that he will be in the opposing ranks soon.

The player in question may have been in the worst form of his life in the run-up to the match and he may not have scored any goals in the last few months leading up to his return, but as soon as he is back on familiar territory he will be banging them in from all angles. This sudden recapturing of form is as gut-wrenching as it is inevitable. The transformation from donkey to world-beater is instantaneous, and of course lasts for just ninety minutes before he returns to type and does not score again throughout the remainder of the season or, in the worst cases, his entire career. A parting shot of such venom would be laughable if it was not so unbearable.

Kevin Phillips is one of those players who strikes fear in the hearts of the fans of his former clubs, of which he has a fair old collection. So when he announced his retirement from playing towards the end of the 2013/14 season, fans from Aston Villa to West Brom must have breathed a huge sigh of relief that he would no longer be inflicting any further pain. Phillips has amassed almost 250 goals, and a fair few of them have been racked up against teams for whom he has played. The most poignant of all his goals against erstwhile employers was the penalty he smashed home in the 2013 Championship play-offs final. Never have I been so certain that a spot kick was going to be dispatched than when Phillips stepped up in extra time to send Palace to the Premier League in place of Watford, Phillips' first professional club. That must have hurt the Hornets fans more than anything else – their favourite son being the one to deliver the knock-out blow, under the gaze of 40,000 agonised fans.

How cruel, but how typical it is of the ex-factor to twist the knife in this manner. Even the most naïve scriptwriter would never have dreamed of creating such a far-fetched denouement. Naturally, the last goal in Phillips' twenty-year career was scored for Leicester City against Blackpool, another of his former clubs. The fact that he seems to take so little pleasure in this makes it much worse. It would be much more acceptable if the player in question was a hateful, obnoxious figure, but Phillips seems such a decent bloke that there is a sneaking admiration for his exploits. He is just doing his job – a little too well, perhaps, but that is his métier, damn his eyes.

Y is for Yellow Boots

> Maybe that's why I'm partly yellow. It's no excuse, though. It really isn't. What you should be is not yellow at all.
>
> From *The Catcher in the Rye* by J. D. Salinger

Well, to be more precise, luminous yellow with purple streaks and nausea-inducing names such as 'Hyper Venom', 'Nitrocharge' or 'Predator'. Someone needs to remind the likes of Nike and Adidas that these are football boots, not lethal spiders, explosive devices or an animal at the upper end of the food chain. No, they are simply football boots, nothing more, nothing less. The predominance of ridiculously coloured footwear has reached epidemic proportions, and watching any match leads to the eyes being assaulted with a garish collection that would not look out of place in an Ibiza club at the height of the summer.

Just to underline the point, recently spotted in *Match of the Day* magazine was quite possibly a contender for the worst item of clothing ever seen in broad daylight: a camouflage boot. It is difficult to understand the rationale behind such a monstrosity. Having insisted that my son is only allowed to wear black boots while playing, it has become increasingly more difficult to find any boots that are not luminous lime or sparkling sapphire. The only concession made was to allow him to have bright green laces.

The blame can be laid at the feet of Alan Ball and Alan Hinton, who bucked the uniformity of black boots during the 1970s by donning their infamous white ones. After the dam had burst, we were then flooded with the technicoloured nightmares of today, albeit four decades on. Ball may have won the World Cup with England and been part of an amazing Everton midfield that dominated English League football, but he has an ineradicable stain on his boots. Similarly, Hinton may have been the lynchpin in Clough's extraordinary Derby County team in the early seventies, winning two League championships, but 'Gladys', as he was affectionately known by Derby fans, will be forever associated with breaking the mould of regulation black boots.

In an interview with the *Star* in 2011, Hinton revealed the reasoning behind his switching from black to white. 'The background to me wearing them was simple,' he explained. 'A company called Hummel approached me and offered me a grand. That was a fair bit of money then. I thought Cloughie would crucify me, but he didn't for some reason.' And we talk about the modern-day footballer being a mercenary. But Hinton's motives were pretty black-and-white.

These two titans of the game have now had their esteemed reputation tarnished, because we can trace the evolution of garish, inappropriate footwear to their breaking the shackles of conformity. There is a trail of shame that leads us to the point of no return when Luis Suárez donned the 'Samba Primeknit', the very first pair of 'knitted' boots, against Manchester United in March 2014. Naturally Suárez scored at Old Trafford, claiming the first 'knitted goal', and followed it up with three goals against Cardiff the following weekend; this was perhaps the world's inaugural 'knit-trick'. Ultimately, that is what should be writ large on his tombstone, in between the biting, diving and handball incidents.

Not only is this a travesty of design, but also, these little monsters retail at an eye-popping £220. Over £200 for a pair of boots. Now we are surely off to hell in a handcart, and that handcart will undoubtedly be lined by shocking pink interiors with a crochet finish. Next stop is oblivion, but that destination would be preferable to the land where these boot manifestations abound and strive to outdo themselves for outlandish, unnatural colours adorned by wholly inappropriate names.

Another 'revolution' in boot design that has been foisted onto the unsuspecting public is the Nike Magista, which was launched with the rather terrifying strapline of 'Football will never be the same'. No, it certainly will not, and the reason why is that the Magista is basically a sock masquerading as a boot. With its flyknit upper and Dynamic Fit collar, it delivers a sock-like fit. So for all of those who have temporarily lost their boot during a match and have had to hop around in a stockinged foot, that is the sensation that Nike are looking for. Uncomfortable and unprotected, you may cry, but do not worry; there is a special waterproof layer, to remind you that you are actually wearing a pair of boots rather than a fancy pair of stockings.

We have also been assailed by Ronaldo's boots, which are modestly called Mercurial IX and feature 'an all-over digital print of the Star Vela Supernova including a seven-star path print', as you do. To top it all off, 'the supernova print is juxtaposed with a chrome swoosh flecked with silver fleck and a Blue Glow outline'. These little beauties/booties actually glow in the dark, and the extraordinary attention to designer detail would not look out of place within the environs of catwalks in Milan, Paris or New York. When boots are launched as though they are part of the latest space mission, we need to stand back and take stock, because we are hurtling towards the nearest death star in a searing blaze of garish galactico glitter.

The other player who has dominated the world stage, alongside Ronaldo, is the less flashy Lionel Messi. But even the more modest man from Rosario has had to succumb to the headlong rush to outsparkle his rival at Real. When Messi overtook the long-standing Barcelona scoring record of Paulino Alcántara with his 371st goal, the limited edition 'Messi 371' boots were being prepared for take-off. Breaking a record that has stood for almost ninety years should obviously be commemorated, but the novelty behind this pair was that were that they were sequin-coated; they could have been inspired by Liberace, Prince and Lady Gaga, all rolled into one rather louche slipper.

Things have come to a pretty pass when a player donning a pair of simple black boots stands out from the crowd as some sort of freak. Maybe, like most fashionable items, the trend will turn full circle and the plain, unadorned boot will inevitably become the hottest show in town. But, until that moment, we will have to endure more weird and wacky designs along the Milky Way and will need to remind ourselves that we have not actually been transported to a distant planet. We are just watching a game of football.

Naturally, most of the attention is drawn towards what is on top of the boot, in all its sparkling, iridescent pomp. But the most important element, the 'engine room', is what is on the underside of the boot. Yet again, here is where fashionable trends seem to have overcome clear, cool, rational thought. The evolution of blades replacing studs is a further cause for concern, not only because it takes a further step towards globalisation of the game but also because these blades do not actually do their job in providing sufficient grip to stay on one's feet. It is quite common to see players losing their footing regularly, sliding and slithering across the surface. To adapt Brain Clough's quote, 'If God had wanted us to play football in blades, he would have put Astroturf down here.' As a result, where balance and poise were previously the name of the game, there is now imbalance and pose.

Y is for Yesterday's Men

> The timeless in you is aware of life's timelessness;
> and knows that yesterday is but today's memory and
> tomorrow is today's dream.
>
> From *The Prophet* by Kahlil Gibran

Football careers are, by their very nature, short-lived. For every Ryan Giggs, there are hundreds of players who leave the game well before they reach thirty. Only so many can end up in coaching or managing positions, and the rest scrabble around to pick up the odd bit of punditry; yet again, however, there are only a finite amount of opportunities available, and once they are established they are difficult to budge. Just look at how long Mark Lawrenson has survived. One way of extending this fragile lifestyle is to move abroad and play in what can loosely be termed a less taxing environment.

Damien Duff has spent time at the top with the likes of Chelsea and Newcastle, and is now facing the autumn of his career. The Irish winger's statement that he was leaving for sunnier climes is a classic statement of denial.

It is a little sad to watch how old pros such as Duff defend their decision, as if it is something about a new challenge rather than one last ride along the gravy train. 'I'll be leaving Fulham,' Duff said. 'I've looked at the Australia or America thing – it would be a different way of life, a different league; I think life's too short just to be stuck in the rat race, if that's the right phrase, over here, so I'd maybe like to taste something new.' The desire to explore other cultures may not be quite as high up the list of priorities as another few grand in the bank account.

Numerous players in their dotage have ended up in exotic locations, and they are quite entitled to ply their trade in the more obscure football outposts. To suggest, for example, that Robbie Fowler turning out for Muang Thong United in the Thai Premier League a few years ago was for anything other than the last lucrative contract is preposterous.

Don Revie was one of the first British football managers to go abroad to seek his fortune, and his abandoning of England in 1977 for the delights of the Gulf were viewed with the utmost suspicion. So incensed were the authorities that he was charged with bringing the game into disrepute by an indignant Football Association. Revie's reputation was irreparably damaged, and anyone following in his path would be viewed with similar levels of suspicion when the main motivation is so clearly and exclusively to do with financial gain, and nothing else.

Z is for Zips

We also have a few problems on the bench – Arsene can't do up the zip on his coat!

Ivan Gazidis, Arsenal chief executive at the Annual General Meeting, 2013

When Whitcomb L. Judson invented the zip fastener in Chicago in 1890, he could not have foreseen the havoc he was going to wreak on the world of football. Zips have been a constant source of frustration and contempt ever since their ignominious entrance. Just ask Arsene Wenger, who has struggled manfully with the zip on his 'caterpillar coat' throughout his long, illustrious (*sic*) reign at Arsenal. The longest serving-manager in the Premier League just cannot get his professorial head around this infernal contraption. However hard he tries, it just gets worse and worse, and the sight of Wenger pulling and tugging at the offending zip has become one of those defining visions of the English winter. Damn your infernal invention, Judson. Just look at the harm you have brought to one of the most revered figures in football. Maybe Arsene could pick up some tips from a higher authority on the most effective way to solve his eternal discomfort, such as Gunnersaurus (see 'M is for Mascots').

Over the 1,000-plus matches Wenger has been in charge of at Arsenal, the zip has become the bane of his life, as well as that of all those watching. It should not be beyond the wit of a man in his mid-sixties, one whose scholarly approach to football earned him the nickname of 'Le Professeur', to possess the required motor skills to do up his zip, or maybe even just get some Velcro to help him out. But on it goes, one man's futile struggle against the zip, and it reached such a level of embarrassment that it was rumoured that official kit supplier Puma were asked to intervene to enable a free-flowing, smoother zip. Maybe Arsenal's legendary parsimony has forced a rethink, and it is Hobson's choice as to whether you get a world-class striker or we get you some buttons for that ruddy coat. The only people who can possibly gain from this impasse are the subeditors, who can revel in a stream of headlines from 'Zip it, Arsene' to 'Button it, Wenger'. At least someone is happy.

Some have suggested that his clear frustration with said item dates back to Arsenal's relative lack of success since 2005. This zip phobia was perhaps symptomatic of his team's inability to replicate the success of his first 500 games, when Arsenal carried all before them, winning three Premier League titles – including the unbeaten season of 2003/04 – and four FA Cups. As their FA Cup triumph over Hull in 2014 brought an end to the

7. Here is Arsene Wenger caught in the never-ending, perpetual struggle with his zip. The harder he tries, the worse it gets.

drought, one can only hope and pray that this will also be the time when the zip issue is resolved once and for all, for everyone's sakes. Or maybe the club, in their moment of glory, could get him that much-needed new zip-free coat.

Even before Wenger's endless wrangling proved the zip has no place in football, some bright spark came up with the notion that zips could be introduced into the standard football shirt. *Quel désastre*, we all muttered under our Gallic breaths. Back in 1998 Manchester United unveiled their thirteenth different shirt in the space of five years, but this one was different as it came with a zip collar.

This was so out of the ordinary that, according to the BBC report at the time, they said the collar 'was designed with an anti-lock mechanism to ensure it does not injure other players'. Surely the fact that this shirt required a mechanism to render it safe to wear should have set the alarm bells ringing. A few followed slavishly in their path, and the zip became all the rage for a nanosecond, but thankfully it was soon buried in its rightful place and was not seen again for several years.

The reintroduction came through an unlikely route; it was not the players, not the managers, but this time the referees who suddenly came over all zip-friendly. This made slightly more sense, as the ref does need to carry a certain amount of essential equipment, such as notebook, pencil and red and yellow cards with him to assist in his role, and a zip helps to keep said items from spilling out of their pockets. But the problem is that the zip goes way beyond the call of duty. We now have the over-sized zip, which adorns the official's right breast and looks as though it could accommodate a match programme, a couple of pies, a spare ball and the matchday mascot with room to spare.

For the sake of transparency, it would be good to know what exactly is tucked away in there. In the perpetual search for truth, I did make a couple of enquiries of the elite referees' body, Premier Game Match Officials Limited, for an explanation as to what there is in that mysterious zipped pocket. The official answer was that although it is rarely used, when it is, the pocket houses the rather sinister-sounding 'spare accessories'. Maybe, after Andre Marriner's mistaken-identity gaffe in Arsene Wenger's 1,000th Arsenal match with Chelsea, when he sent off Gibbs rather than Oxlade-Chamberlain, a handy photo album of all the players would be a good idea to save any future embarrassment.

Then again, it might be that Vivienne Westwood has been engaged to design the refs' strips, and we are going back to a late 1970s punk revival to add some street chic to contemporary match officiating. In the future, we could have assistant referees in ripped bondage gear, while those fourth and fifth officials could make their mark in some natty black bin liners. The idea of Phil 'Vicious' Dowd with a barbed-wire tattoo across his neck could bring some spice to Monday night football. Next up, 'Mad' Mark Clattenburg in ripped trousers and with a safety pin through his nose, as Adam Lallana chirps away in his ear, 'But you have changed so much since you got that new outfit, Clatters.' Now that's an image to conjure up and then consign to the bin – minus the liners, naturally.

Z is for Z-List Celebrities

Celebrity is a mask that eats into the face.
From *Self-Consciousness: Memoirs* by John Updike

You know the score; a team makes it to their first Cup final in ages, and then out come the celebrity fans, one by one, declaring their undying love for their team. Never mind that such devotion has been hidden under a bushel over the last few years. They will be out in force at Wembley and all over the media, nonchalantly talking about being taken to their first match when they were only five months old, about how much it means to them and how they had never even dreamed of such a day for the Blues – or is it the Reds these days?

The worst culprits are the really minor-league celebrities, who spot the bandwagon rolling past and cannot wait to jump on board for the ride. Z-listers from the bottom drawer of the celebrity wardrobe come rushing forward in a frantic race to be seen. One-hit wonders from the 1990s and actors who once appeared in *Emmerdale* in 2003 for a couple of episodes are back in the limelight, and they are determined to make the most of it because they weren't alive the last time the team reached Wembley in 1931. 'This club has always been a major part of me, and this is the happiest day of my life so far. Well, apart from landing the role as a postman in a couple of episodes in *Emmerdale*, of course.'

When quizzed about how many of the earlier rounds of the Cup run they might have been to, unfortunately there has always been a clash because of the endless stream of auditions, but the diary has been blocked off for that date in May and nothing will get in the way. Apart from if that long-awaited *Coronation Street* call comes through. But they will definitely record the match, or maybe catch the highlights later; whatever happens, they will be there in spirit, cheering on the lads.

Consequently, with Hull City's first appearance in an FA Cup final in their 110-year existence, it was no surprise to see a few long-lost fans crawling out of the woodwork. Diehard fan Sinitta, she of *The X-Factor*, *The Jump* and a string of minor hits through the 1980s, was seen espousing the Hull cause and wearing the Hull shirt (no, not that one – see 'K is for Kit') everywhere she went. This comment on a Hull supporters' message board sums it up. 'I know Sinitta is a Chelsea fan, but she watches out for our results. I know, it's hardly A-list, but it's one.' How desperate and pitiful is that? They're accepting that she supports another club, a bigger club, but still claiming her as one of their own. Being an unfashionable club from Humberside, they don't attract enough stars, so there is an appropriation of other clubs' supporters to embellish the ranks of Tigers-supporting celebs. There is really one way to sum up that sort of painful pursuit of celebrity endorsement. Grrrrr. For pity's sake, stop.

Conclusion

> For hate is not conquered by hate: hate is conquered by love. This is a law eternal.
>
> From *Dhammapada*, early Buddhist sacred text

And so, we have reached the end of our journey, having picked our way through the maze of football hates from a variety of angles. Along the way we have encountered beasts and behemoths, the disenfranchised and the omnipotent, the laughable and the lamentable. All of them have their place in the firmament. Some will have irked you mildly, while others will have sent you into a raging fit of pique. Some will pale into insignificance over the coming years, while others will become ever more annoying, to the point at which a mere glimpse inspires paroxysms of rage. There will be a host of new ones that crop up, as well as old ones that will come back to haunt us.

Such is the power of emotion engendered by football that, through all these many frustrations, there is one constant, and this is that the more we love the game the more we hate aspects of it.

Just as Jane Austen wrote of her eponymous heroine Emma Woodhouse that she loved her, despite her manifest faults, so do I feel about football. And football may be tainted, it may be crammed full with imperfections and packed with some of the more sinister characters in sport, but it still remains the beautiful game, which we all love very deeply.

The list of hates will change, evolve and develop, so hopefully future editions of this book will reflect this. I encourage you all to keep a note of these as they crop up, and please add or amend through the website (www.azfootballhates.co.uk) as well as through social media. Do feel free to tweet your own choices to @rcfoster. Keep them coming thick and fast, and purge yourself of those inner demons. After all, I managed to reduce my original eighty-seven down to a much more manageable forty-one.

There is, however, one final hate that did not make the original selection, because it is almost too intense and so far-reaching that it sullies any enjoyment of football. But on reflection, after finishing the book, I could not allow it to pass by unnoticed. It makes me cringe and cry simultaneously, and, as we learned in 'C is for Crying', seeing a grown man reduced to a blubbering wreck is not pleasant. But I do feel that it is my painful duty to draw attention to it, and it is particularly poignant on the eve of another season, which I look forward to with a curious combination of anticipation and apprehension.

This particular bugbear will be a continuous feature of the action for the next ten months. This is guaranteed to do your head in, and your football viewing (whether it be live or on television) will be blighted with this particular assault on our senses; if you do not want to have your attention drawn to it, look away now, as they say on the Saturday night news.

Whichever bright spark, marketing guru or advertising visionary dreamed up this abominable idea should be hunted down and locked in a dark cell for several years while having sharp pins inserted into their eyes, in order to mirror our own deeply unpleasant sensory experience. This piece of nonsense is all the worse for being ubiquitous; it is always there, but never wanted. It could be argued that there are worse things in the world, but I am hard pressed to think of any at this moment that are quite so insidious and damaging.

It is quite simply the ever revolving advertising that has engulfed the perimeter boards at grounds. The Premier League hailed the pioneering technology a few years ago without any sense of shame: 'We've seen advances such as electronic signboards that can flash, change and rotate advertising messages during a game.' Very clever, but if this is progress then call me a Luddite, because I have an uncontrollable urge to smash all these boards one by one into the tiniest of smithereens. This new way of pumping messages directly into our consciousness is not just infuriatingly distracting but, much to my eternal frustration, it actually becomes compulsive viewing. Once you get drawn into its world it is almost impossible to escape. It is partly down to the fluorescent colours that sear our eyeballs, and partly the flickering motion that makes it such unrelenting, horrible viewing. At the very least, there should be a disclaimer along the lines of 'these bastards are going to ruin your afternoon or evening and drive you to the edge of despair'.

The worst aspect is that the majority of these ads feature the very things that have formed the subject matter of this book. Maybe it is an inducement to join the fun in Qatar 2022, or perhaps having the new Samba pre-knit being forced down our throats and on to our children's feet, or the next clarion call to place bets throughout the course of the match. Increasingly, among all this detritus, there will be the variety of messages aimed at the all-important Asian market, delivered in Chinese characters, which may contain dark secrets – but how will we ever know, unless they start providing subtitles? From kick-off to final whistle, there is simply no respite from this full frontal assault on our senses.

When the inevitable gambling ads start churning over and over and the desperate plea to put a wager on the next scorer actually scrolls behind the shoulder of the very same player, it is surely time to call a halt. We cannot be far away from the next stage, where the ads will be superimposed on the players' shirts, and, as they prepare to shoot, the odds will be displayed in the blink of any eye or a swipe of the left foot. It is certainly at this moment that we will know we have reached rock bottom and that we will be stuck in a perpetual loop of shame. A nadir of such bleakness, one that leaves us so bereft of hope, can only be faced with the knowledge that the person responsible is in perpetual pain in a dungeon somewhere several miles beneath the earth's crust and will never be allowed to resurface. This bubble of depravity envelops us, and it renders what should be a simple game of football into an orgy of advertising messages and sponsors' taglines, all piled on top of us, the poor unsuspecting public.

To end on a positive note, and taking inspiration from the American civil rights movement of the 1960s, which refused to lie down and accept the status quo: we shall overcome. But everyone needs to be on their guard to halt the rise of this insidious menace and preserve the game we love from the choking, cloying influence of these LED invaders. If we do not provide stiff resistance, then our fate is sealed; we will have let ourselves down and failed future generations of fans. We all have an individual as well as a collective responsibility, which cannot be shirked. There can be no excuses, no second chances; judgement day has arrived, and these outrageous displays of commercialisation have to go as soon as possible.

On the guiding principle that it is better out than in, I do hope that sharing in *What I Hate about Football* has allowed you to release some pent-up emotion. Bottling up years of vexation and torment can be harmful, so this book represents a golden opportunity to rid yourself of those suppressed feelings once and for all. By acknowledging and admitting to those negative thoughts, you should now feel liberated to move on and enjoy your football more freely. My own passion for the game has grown even stronger through the process of researching, compiling and writing about the myriad of hates that have been bugging us for so long and which will continue to do so. Lest we forget, through hate our love grows stronger.

Acknowledgements

I owe a debt of gratitude to many people for their help, assistance and advice with writing and compiling this book. I cannot mention them all by name, but I wanted to take this opportunity to highlight a few I wanted to express my thanks to formally.

First and foremost a special mention goes to Phil Morgan. He spent many selfless hours helping with illustrations before we snatched defeat from the jaws of victory by ultimately having to plump for plain reproduction, but Phil deserves recognition for his efforts. As a matter of interest, Phil's pet hate is the current vogue among certain spectators of capturing the action on their iPad, which is indeed a worrying trend. Thanks also go to Laura Wagg at PA Images, who rescued us when time was tight.

Secondly, the wide range of people from all walks of life who have contributed to the book by providing their own football hates. Everyone who is featured here gave willingly and promptly of their time and words, with the resulting compilation providing an excellent perspective on the topic. Nearly all of them were also extremely positive about the concept behind the book and gave timely lifts to my spirits when they might have been flagging. I must also point out that I did approach a fair number of women to contribute, but unfortunately none of them accepted; it is therefore exclusively a male viewpoint, but not by design.

There have also been a fair few friends who have acted as invaluable mentors, encouraging me when I needed it most and keeping me in check when I was getting carried away. A special thanks goes to Matt, who acted as my mentor and who was instrumental in getting this book off the ground. Peter Whitehead, Ben Lyttleton, Gus Hurdle and Simon London are all worth a mention for their continuing support and wise words, especially during the more challenging moments.

Jon Jackson, Publishing Director at Amberley, has proved to be a steady hand and has let me get on with writing with minimal interference.

Finally, a massive thanks to my family. My wife Yvonne and children Jessica, Amelia and Tristram have had to put up with my obsessive behaviour over the last few months, and have given me the strength to meet my deadlines without a murmur of complaint. This book is dedicated to you.

Richard Foster
3 July 2014.

ALSO AVAILABLE FROM AMBERLEY PUBLISHING

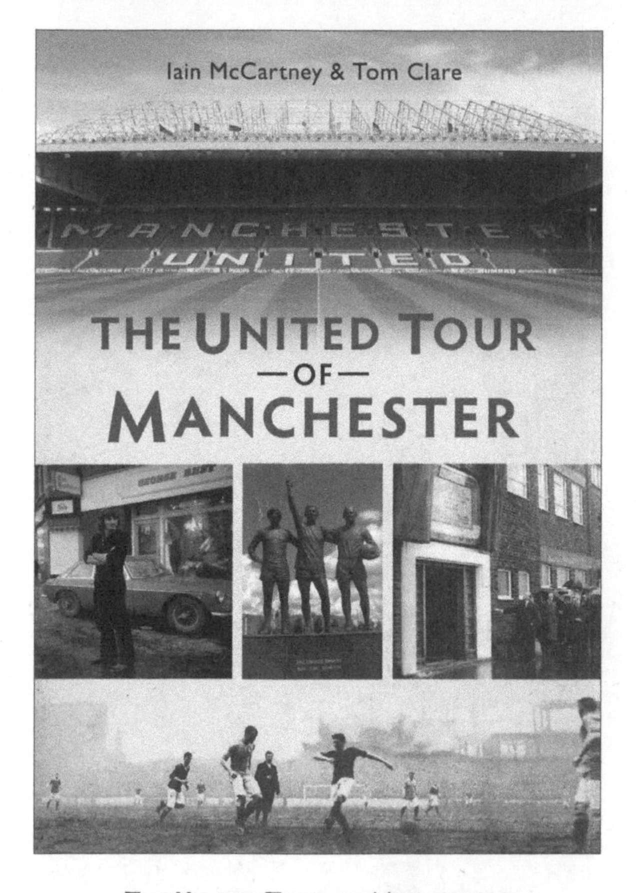

THE UNITED TOUR OF MANCHESTER

Iain McCartney & Tom Clare

Ever wondered what the connection between Manchester United and Bramhall Hall is? Do you know the exact location where the Professional Footballers Association was founded? Where does the first captain of Manchester United to lift a major trophy lie at rest? The answers are to be found in this book, which takes you on the United Tour of Manchester.

978 1 4456 1913 2
128 pages, full colour

Available from all good bookshops or order direct from our website www.amberleybooks.com